Rhapsody and Redolence

"When I saw Carol Scott's paintings, my first impression was their wondrous intensity—bursting with joy! The colors are shockingly bold, and the things in the painting feel like they are in motion. For me, her art expresses both movement and stillness, almost shouting with gladness. Because of its subject matter—I am thinking here specifically of 'Luminous Mysteries,' but all her works have this element—her art shimmers with profundity, as Scott seems to have penetrated into the deepest energy and passion that pours forth from Christ's cross. I can't think of other artists whose works pulsate with the joy and energy of being, and with the 'pouring forth' or shouting with joy of sheer grace, that I find in Scott's best paintings, of which there are many."

—MATTHEW LEVERING,
chair of theology, University of Saint Mary of the Lake

"This book is unique. Punctuated by Carol Scott's intriguing drawings and her mostly co-authored poems, Caitlin Smith Gilson's life-shaping themes feature God, sex, death, surrender, time, art, love, prayer, and suffering. Her constant awareness of finitude, 'every day is the last day of our lives,' and her fascination with time and death is offset by an overflowing sense of erotic and mystical abundance where the worldly and unworldly blend in an outpouring of challenging, impressionistic poems: 'Ravenous for living / She writes like breathing air / With perfumed words of wafted wisdom.'"

—MICHEAL O'SIADHAIL,
poet, author of *The Five Quintets* and *Desire*

"Here, betwixt word and image, is found a singular invitation to dance and wrestle, to die and come alive—all at once—in rhythmic meter to an existential psalter that captures the simultaneity of transcendence and immanence. Here is the explosion of contradistinctions and the unearthing of the hidden givenness of being as true gift, revealing the *analogia entis* as the deeper grammar sustaining and articulating reality as such. Carol Scott's evocative pieces image this grammar in the haunting beauty of fragility, vulnerability, that refracts the infinite array of grace given and received, drawing the gaze in and so through to a deeper reckoning with what stands beyond, while Caitlin Smith Gilson's raw, unadulterated style unerringly traces the very contours of existence, thickly felt beyond the mere gesturing of words, thus embodying a decisive voice beyond words: a true philo-sopher. Together, they unveil that the center exists precisely at the periphery, and that totality can only ever be glimpsed in part. *Rhapsody and Redolence* is nothing less than the human condition on full display."

—JOSEPH TERRY,
co-founder and managing director, Sophia

"*Rhapsody and Redolence* is an astonishing achievement. This collaboration between poet-philosopher Caitlin Smith Gilson and artist Carol Scott issues in a text of extraordinary ambition and deep experiential excavation of the largest themes imaginable—for example, God, death, sacrifice, time, and suffering as these are expressed in a language that is simultaneous cry and prayer, scream of pain and joy, soundings of the inarticulate and word and image perfectly realized. This is an interpenetration of image and word that points to their impossible union that is a height and a depth, a participation in what is beyond that allows the below to shine. As the word 'decade' in the title suggests, the poems and images move towards a condition of prayer. If the note sounded is that of desire, ecstasy, and the holding and withholding of release, the tone is sensuous, sensual, bespeaking a carnality that makes human beings more rather than less than angels. This volume is unnervingly and relentlessly raw as it speaks again and again to the caress, to its promise, and to the twinned bodies of lovers, mortal and immortal. The love intimated is violent and equally terrible whether we are speaking of human lovers or our love for God and God's ravenous love for us. One of the extraordinary features of the text is that the sensuality of the text never allows the distance of allegory. The mutual love of human beings (at their depth) and God, who is depth as well as height, is as sensual and enfleshed as the love between a woman and a man. Though the violence of love cannot be constrained, nonetheless, it is eucharistic in that we are speaking of the sharing of the saving gift of everything we have even up to the limit of what we don't have. In any event, the sharing is what brings us into being by way of becoming, though both are founded by the event of an unanticipated approach. The voicing in the poem is unique. It is redolent of the brave casualness of Donne and Herbert before Eliot's so-called 'dissociation of sensibility,' while also inescapably evocative of medieval women mystics such as Angela of Foligno waiting on rapture. But the casualness is now more brazen and the key even more fevered in the nonchalance attending the language of arousal and consummation. This is a brilliant book that makes the darkness shine through the body that has become the sensorium of transcendence. It is a book of poetry that explodes verse by exploring its conditions, a book of philosophy in that it secures as Merleau Ponty did the body as the site of invisibility and transcendence, and a work in theology—evoking the thought of John Paul II—insofar as it shows that a bore into our carnality is always through it to a lightning core that enables our relation to God to exceed our desire, even as it grounds it."

—CYRIL O'REGAN,
professor of theology, University of Notre Dame

"To encounter Carol Scott's art is to know that strange exhilaration of stepping through an overlooked door on a familiar street and into a world vertiginous, enchanting, alive to the ceaseless throb of wonder. By turns jocund, searing, and prayerful, the work evinces a contemplative vision shot through with all the colors and shades of feeling known to the eyes of childhood. Playfully fluent in the tradition, it nonetheless eludes all facile comparison. Like all great art, it somehow leaves us less certain of our way of being in the world, even as it gives us back a part of ourselves we hadn't yet known to look for."

—DANNY FITZPATRICK,
editor, *Joie De Vivre Quarterly Journal of Arts, Culture, and Letters*

"Poetry that transports me whither I know not. Christianity broken open to all its intrinsically rapturous madness. Piercing and poignant, a rawly sensual poetry that also raises awareness at a theoretical level of the metaphysical underpinnings and resources that make original language possible at the limits of expression. Caitlin Smith Gilson makes immediately palpable in poetry the unthinkable and unsayable that a philosophical understanding of language and its limits can explain in discursive terms only by performative contradiction. I plan to continue to read and treasure this work, which evinces a remarkable but quite unpredictable coherence."

—WILLIAM FRANKE,
professor of comparative literature, Vanderbilt University

"So many things converge in this book that are rarely found together: visual art and poetry, high philosophical reflection and fundamental human feeling, pious contemplation and sensual urgency, and—not least—the original activity of two genuinely creative spirits. The result is indeed an 'exercise in newness' as the author's note proposes, and the reader receives the gift of witnessing truth, goodness, and beauty in the moment of their birth. One is tempted to say the experience is dis-orienting, but the more fitting word is re-orienting—toward the things that matter. We owe the authors a debt of gratitude."

—D. C. SCHINDLER,
professor or metaphysics and anthropology, Pontifical John Paul II Institute for Studies on Marriage and Family

Rhapsody and Redolence

The Crystal Decade

BY CAROL SCOTT
& CAITLIN SMITH GILSON
With Original Art by Carol Scott

Foreword by Steven E. Knepper

▲ CASCADE *Books* • Eugene, Oregon

RHAPSODY AND REDOLENCE
The Crystal Decade

Copyright © 2024 Carol Scott and Caitlin Smith Gilson. All rights reserved. Except for brief quotations in critical publications or reviews, no part of this book may be reproduced in any manner without prior written permission from the publisher. Write: Permissions, Wipf and Stock Publishers, 199 W. 8th Ave., Suite 3, Eugene, OR 97401.

Cascade Books
An Imprint of Wipf and Stock Publishers
199 W. 8th Ave., Suite 3
Eugene, OR 97401

www.wipfandstock.com

PAPERBACK ISBN: 979-8-3852-0230-0
HARDCOVER ISBN: 979-8-3852-0231-7
EBOOK ISBN: 979-8-3852-0232-4

Cataloguing-in-Publication data:

Names: Scott, Carol [author] [artist]. | Smith Gilson, Caitlin [author]. | Knepper, Steven E. [foreword writer].

Title: Rhapsody and redolence : the crystal decade / by Carol Scott and Caitlin Smith Gilson ; with original art by Carol Scott and a foreword by Steven E. Knepper.

Description: Eugene, OR: Cascade Books, 2024.

Identifiers: ISBN 979-8-3852-0230-0 (paperback) | ISBN 979-8-3852-0231-7 (hardcover) | ISBN 979-8-3852-0232-4 (ebook)

Subjects: LCSH: Poetry. | Christian poetry—English. | Religious poetry. | Art—Philosophy. | paintings. | Philosophical theology. | Art and religion.

Classification: PN6110 S36 2024 (paperback) | PN6110 (ebook)

03/14/24
Color Rhapsody—Cover Art, Carol Scott

Contents

Author's Note | xi
        Fallen Down. **Art by Carol Scott** | xx
Foreword by Steven E. Knepper | xxi
        The Last Laugh. **Art by Carol Scott** | xxv
Dedication | xxvi
Acknowledgments | xxvii

I. THE FIRST DECADE: GOD

The Fisher of Men. **Art by Carol Scott** | 2

Maundy Thursday | 3
Christ's Coming | 5
The Falconer | 8
Veni Donum | 10
Thy Will Be Done | 11
The Longior Via | 13
The Untitled | 15
The Interrogative | 17

GOD: THE SHARED POETRY OF ARTIST CAROL SCOTT AND CAITLIN SMITH GILSON

Unstoppable. **Art by Carol Scott** | 20
Requiem | 21
Dreamland | 22
Glory | 23
Sacred Geometry | 24

II. THE SECOND DECADE: SEX

Sweet Treat. **Art by Carol Scott** | 28

The Jackal | 29
Gli Amanti | 30
Dionysius in Time and Space | 32
The Writ | 34
La Petite Mort | 35
El Damasco | 36
My Sweat from the Day of You | 38
The In-Between | 39
I Left My Eyes at Your Door | 40

Sex: The Shared Poetry of Artist Carol Scott and Caitlin Smith Gilson
Pure Life. Art by Carol Scott | 42

Sexy Will Out | 43
Stone Fruit | 44
Seduced by the Sound of You | 46
Experience | 48

III. THE THIRD DECADE: SURRENDER

St. Teresa in Ecstasy. **Art by Carol Scott** | 50

Il Ladro | 51
Chavah | 53
The Armory | 55
Surrender in Spades | 57
Christ's Kiss | 58
Rendering | 61
Ebb Tide | 62
Your Teresa in Ecstasy | 63
Today Is the Last Day | 65
Bend My Heart Around Your Waist | 67
Your Surrender | 69

Surrender: The Shared Poetry of Artist Carol Scott and Caitlin Smith Gilson
Redolent Blue. Art by Carol Scott | 72

Liquid Feeling | 73
IN-timacy | 75
I Surrender to What May Come | 76
Carried | 78

IV. THE FOURTH DECADE: DEATH

Reflections Ice Storm. **Art by Carol Scott** | 82

Come With Me | 83
In Dying Time | 85
Stargazer | 86
Sunday's Catacomb | 89
In the Land of Myth | 91
Un-Ranked | 94
If I Could Haunt You | 96
The Word | 97
Still . . . | 99
The Catalogue | 101

DEATH: THE SHARED POETRY OF ARTIST CAROL SCOTT
AND CAITLIN SMITH GILSON
Lace. **Art by Carol Scott** | 104

Death Is Not the Enemy | 105
The Yielding | 106
There Is Dying Underneath All My Living | 107
Poured Out | 109

V. THE FIFTH DECADE: TIME

Crystal Ball, Tell Us All. **Art by Carol Scott** | 112

Trevignano Across the Way | 113
God between the Lines | 117
The Recollection | 118
The Char | 119
In My Beginning | 121
What Precedes | 122
Calyx | 123
The Wager | 125
In the Time of Unforgiving | 127

TIME: THE SHARED POETRY OF ARTIST CAROL SCOTT
AND CAITLIN SMITH GILSON | 123
Flutes. **Art by Carol Scott** | 123

What I Know for Sure | 131
What Is Your Story? | 132
Life, Death, and Life Again | 134
My Skin Remembers You | 135

VI. THE SIXTH DECADE: ART

Magnum Opus. Art by Carol Scott | 138

The Divine Artist | 139
The Lantern | 142
Il Regalo | 145
The Artist | 148
The Blue | 150
The Visionary in High Contrast | 152
To Paint in Heaven with You | 154
Narcissus in Glass | 156
My Children: The Only Lasting Art | 158

Art: The Shared Poetry of Artist Carol Scott and Caitlin Smith Gilson

Full Throttle. Art by Carol Scott | 160

Her Tumbler of Glass | 161
Art as Food | 163
The Artisan | 165
Writing Partners | 167

VII. THE SEVENTH DECADE: PRAYER

Dome. Art by Carol Scott | 160

The Psalmist's Early Lament | 171
Lines to God before Sleep | 173
Brutish Prayer | 175
A Little Prayer | 178
The Game | 179
The Doubled Prayer | 181
Your Prayer Is Coarse Wood | 183
Only Silence Can I Give | 186

Prayer: The Shared Poetry of Artist Carol Scott and Caitlin Smith Gilson

48 Shades of Crystal. Art by Carol Scott | 188

I Feel More than I See | 189
Pound Me into Your Bronze | 190
Ache | 191
First Soul | 194

VIII. THE EIGHTH DECADE: LOVE

Passion. Art by Carol Scott | 196

I Am Thinking about the Small of Your Back | 197
The Uncollected | 199
Lago di Bracciano | 202
The Incarnate Ecstasy | 204
The Cotswolds, My Love | 205
Of Anzio | 207
Strawberries and Cream | 208
Of Friendship | 209
You Should Know by Now | 211
The Long Now | 212

LOVE: THE SHARED POETRY OF ARTIST CAROL SCOTT
AND CAITLIN SMITH GILSON

Love and Pain. Art by Carol Scott | 214

Holy Coquetry | 215
To Those Who Do Not Know | 216
The Nectar of Sweet Dreams | 219
The Ground of You | 220

IX. THE NINTH DECADE: ROSARY

Full of Grace. Art by Carol Scott | 222

I Dreamt of You | 223
The Shadowless Woman | 224
Virgo Perdolens | 226
Another Fiat | 227
Our Lady Remains | 228
Chara | 230
The Waterfall | 232
Manna | 235

ROSARY: THE SHARED POETRY OF ARTIST CAROL SCOTT
AND CAITLIN SMITH GILSON

Beautiful. Art by Carol Scott | 225

The Rosary | 239
On Christmas Day | 242
Rose of Love | 243
Crystal Fire | 244

X. THE TENTH DECADE: SUFFERING

Honey Island Swamp. Art by Carol Scott | 248

Anguillara | 249
Descend into Memory | 252
Cours | 255
In the Wonderland of Lamentation | 256
Love Among the Ruins | 258
Thirteen | 261
Artifact | 263
Algorithms of Imitation | 264
My Needy Heart I Weep | 265
I Will Never Love Like This Again | 266
God I Miss You | 267

Suffering: The Shared Poetry of Artist Carol Scott
and Caitlin Smith Gilson
Pushed and Pinned. Art by Carol Scott | 270

The Ramparts | 271
Seventy Seven | 272
War on Me | 273
Despair | 275

LAGNIAPPE | 279

The Big Catch. Art by Carol Scott | 264

Innamorati | 281
Sleep in Hiding | 282
Sempre | 284
Advice for the Broken Hearted | 286
Banana Moon | 287
The Whitened Tear | 289
Unmapped | 292
Purgatory | 293
The Light Is Too Bright | 294
Another Theban Cycle | 295

Night Heron. Art by Carol Scott | 301

POSTSCRIPT | 303

Pieta | 304

Our Lady of Souls. Art by Carol Scott | 305

The Authors | 306

Author's Note
Among the Wraiths of Poetry

THE POET STANDS AT THE PORTICO as experience is read *through* her. This is a gate where entrance does not afford exit. At times, it is a low door where the torrent of pressured water is rushing through. As intensively imitative of creation, the poet must remain affixed to each corner of the doorway, taking on what flows relentlessly past her body, and through her appetitive inclination. She is not asked to direct the water.

In this precarity of flesh and spirit, image precedes word and threatens to overwhelm and to disjoin thought from time. Yet, finding each sacrificial word, as *meson* or measure, to sculpt the union threatens to shorten and intensify the protracted dying within all human living. In essence, the very real, sometimes hieratic poetic act, is the originary in-dwelling and the event horizon of all philosophical and theological contemplation. The poetic—I did *not* say poetry—must be experienced if we are to know. Etienne Gilson once aphoristically remarked that we become thinkers when we ruin ourselves as knowers. The poetic, as body and soul debriding the other into its more unified form, *is* the knowing that encounters temporality truly. Not as chronological happening but as moment, presence, full thereness, the sensual climax, as inexhaustibly yet fleetingly, more than sex—the *arche* and *eschaton* of thinking about Being and God.

The poet need not claim to understand fully the nuance, depth, and direction of the tide that engulfs and recedes from her being, but this very transfixion, the sometimes brutal, and sometimes gentle, honesty and lucidity of it, *is* the testament to the sheerly given mystery. This *poesis* is the moment when mouth must open and nothing but the rare, fearsome, undiluted *eros* and *agape*—Truth preceding truths, Goodness preceding the various goods, and the Beautiful preceding the many beautiful things—must enter into concord with Being, as the very faces of Being.

Who can endure that doorway for long? It demands a theotic madness from its willing and transparentized victim—the bones are made as silk, the skin no longer coverall. . . .

The truth about language is that it can only exist to reverse the order of experience and yet experience is what we seek to reenact in language. Our speaking hides the very event we seek to re-experience in language. Most of the time—and as it should be—we communicate oblivious to this universal oddity. We create our own chessboards in language. Each owns the Queen and moves at will. Daily language is a plaything picked up and put down—declarative sentences, decorative conversation, annoyances expressed—and we are its un-examining victors.

Language does fail us at times. The death howl, the falling to one's knees at the violent mortal stripping of the beloved other, that bloodshed Banshee-scream against dying. What is voiced resides below or above word, and certainly cannot get into word. It stands outside word as disarticulated jaw from skull. This failing to communicate communicates. The death howl will not sully itself with the wrong word, with the plaything, and so it leaves itself, it heaves itself, into wordless lamentation. But who can or wants to endure such communication? While honest in existential order—the experience *is* the guttering wildness—it is lethal all the same.

The reality below this reversal of experience and language does intrude. When we communicate by artifice, our daily words exile and make a ghost of actual experience. But all ghosts do what specters do—haunt the other. The torrent on the other side of the closed doorway will trespass, and no amount of checkmating will prevent the watershed. Visceral non-mediated experience does not play by the rules of the construct or the language game. It is the game of all games, Plato's deadly serious game.

The human person is ill-equipped to rectify the relentless dilution of experiential authenticity. We have words, and words will fail us, they inevitably lessen the experience, pervert the order, remove the layers of intensity or inversely cover the shivering nudity at hand. With words, it is never the right pitch, we sing the wrong note and wrong tune most of our lives. All the while the right pitch, the right tune, and the right note lay beside us as we sleep, and we feel it more than our own estate. This paradoxical unease harkens back to civilizational foundation, to the interiority of family bond, friendship, even lovers: there must be this setting aside of the very power of word *to be* matched experience, in order to carry on with the business of life. For word to live at the level of experience, *as* the encounter itself, as flesh and soul trembling on the stem, about to fall, we would have to be gods, and at the totalizing whim of gods. We would have to carry contradiction as union, utterly irreducible to death and entirely made for suffering, for ecstasy. We would have to become an unarmed weeping forth of life itself and yet the very torrent coming through our own doorway.

THE ARTIST AND THE POET

This work began as an abyss calling forth its own, deep calls forth deep, as lamb, lion, deer, and serpent come to the river's embankment and gauge the other. At certain times, the river may be where John baptizes Christ, or the fetid waters dividing the Inferno; it may be the springs of blessed forgetting, or the all too earthly rapids, too cold or too warm, never quite home. The philosopher must always begin from a homeless thought of unvarnished truth. This rough singular thought working against the grain of one's body and soul, impresses its pattern into daily life until cohesion arrives. But on rare occasions, the philosopher must go farther still. The unvarnished truth does not make an appearance, it refuses the thinker, and she languishes in waitingness unsure whether she is barren or alongside the font of fecundity. The unkempt Transcendent lays in wait for her, her own *apocalypsis*, along the river *lethe*. To philosophize, she must engage the emblematic animals of Being, those that howl, and lay down at their sides, or have no legs but crawl with dirtied scaled stomach. The philosopher must recover the poetic, she must *be* as these spirits, must take on the ardor of their perfume and their decomposition, overwhelmed in smell and taste, a carnal *synesthesia* confused of spirit. The truth has not come via presence, it has come through *absence* in midnight forest or in blinding sun, but it is always too much to handle and to assimilate.

Should the philosopher want to philosophize again, then this is the road to be traveled, thought needs raw unmanageable experience. Ordered thought dies without the first eventful taste of time briefly eclipsing Being, and Being thrusting time back down into supplication. Without this confrontation, the very measure of humans as the horizon between time and eternity, closer to angels, but neither angel nor fully animal, our thinking becomes ideological and self-enclosed patterns of attrition. Due to the reversal of order, of daily word acting as if it can lead experience, we reside dangerously too near this great lie, we flirt with it daily. The human existent is always a split hair away from the kind of thinking that will never have the power to kill Being but may have the power to close off our access. Should that occur, as it is occurring now, we may become all too human—a more determinative descent of the fall. That would be the greatest cause for sighing and gnashing of teeth, but the only ones left to weep would be the angels or the demons among us, neither of whom have the flesh to quake or the blood to cleanse the tabernacle of Word made Flesh.

This *poesis* envisions a virginal and timeless way of engagement, a renewed ancient dwelling as radical philosophy. These poetic cycles are an excavation of the *radices* or roots radiating underneath meaning and experience *through* a transportive or brought-experience. The poet is brought by experience into word *as* un-mediated experience. The position of the intellectual spectator is surrendered in favor of the experiential Transcendentals as reified. The Transcendentals are always new, and always capable of astonishing the heart and mind, because they are what is most interior: they are present before we wake; before we know our desires; they are present when we fall in love; they are present when our bodies soften and weaken; they are present even when we deny the other in the long line of historical Judases; they are present when we forget our names; and they are present as the stroking hand when our head lays on the lap of the other.

The ten cycles of poetry—God, Sex, Surrender, Death, Time, Art, Prayer, Love, Rosary, Suffering—intend a *new* kind of philosophical and theological thinking. Here, the poet begins from the unrepeatable courtship with the intimate new, with the blushed and chaste forever-firsts of existence as Truth, Goodness, and Beauty in *actus*. The contrasting tensions of lostness, disease, ugliness, obscurity, disintegration dominate and appear to oppose the Transcendentals, but are the necessary purgative force, the entrance into the human-and-divine *eros* through stretched ecstatic suffering. This purgative all-enclosing encompassing demand evokes the essential homelessness where agapeic abnegation seeks, relentlessly to its death, the lover and beloved union. It will seek nothing lesser; it *cannot* seek anything more, it seeks love, but be warned, it is no plaything. It is love that demands, cautions, invites, tosses ships, takes souls apart as if they were bodies. In fact, in this new kind of philosophizing, love is the architect of the game. The poet has no chance of winning against the designer who can remove the pieces, due to rules being uncovered that she has not yet learned, but will learn as she is surrendered, as she is lost.

It is always fads that are old and uncreative. The relentless search for creativity is part of the glory and folly of the human condition and can lead the artist or poet down into intellectual dishonesty and ideological terror. This is a collection at the coal mouth of divine utterance, it engages the place where paths begin, before the path is trod, at the first step of being trod, where word is fleshed with wisdom. To accomplish this new kind of thinking—a resolutely freed-from-fad, radical originary philosophy—the poet had to begin as all beginnings do: within the face of the other, honest, stripped of guile and pretense.

The poet found her *other* in the exceptional New Orleans artist Carol Scott, who plays with reflection and light, particularly how the gaze of one is remade in the face of the other. Carol's artistic legacy is her intensive and mystic devotion to the naked naturalness of first appearances. She explores how things first come together in light and sight, what recedes and remains underneath as compared to what presents itself, what is demarcated into shadow and what bares itself in light, and more, how to accentuate one's perception of that light in simple objects. Most suggestively, she utilizes magnificent unadulterated color as the primal basis of image, understanding color within the lain image *before* experience, *before* the experienced-word, *before* that word is re-articulated in poetic form. Color, for Carol, evokes the first and immediate touching, sighting, tasting, hearing, perfume of divine presence within the unrepeatability of person in his or her world. Color captures all the senses, including the interior senses that unite spirits, drawing beings out of themselves into the luminosity that invites transcendence. Color transmuted into an infinity of reflection is, for the artist, the very template of experience, and the secret foundation for every word vested in the precarity of flesh and wholly divested of reductive abstraction.

This collection as exercise in newness, in radical philosophy, revolves around its dynamic, entirely novel, but indispensable approach. The process is vital prolonged engagement with the *other* you engage as creation, and who engages you as her creation, each producing self-as-other. It is the proper *doing* of philosophy as betrothed to wonder; wonder that is both alluring and haunting, and because of a balance of power and vulnerability, one is simultaneously creator being created, and creating from that creation. It is an orbit of intensified knowing oneself through the gaze of the other who is known through you.

As poet, I grounded the present "now" in a mirrored reflection on Carol's art; the writings were anchored in the statured image, in the brilliance of unfettered colors captivating the senses, arresting thought, so the poetic heart remained for a moment in agonic stillness, in the in-between of all things. This experience of the truer philosopher is the hidden *metaxy* situated at the height of *eros* right before the surrender into *agape*, right at the top of the seesaw, between up and down, between ecstasy and suffering, between living and dying. It is the experience where a human can justly be like God, and be all things while also being resolutely mortal. Remaining faithful to the art as meditative medium meant the *poesis* held in right pitch within the artist's crystalline dimensions which reside thoroughly outside and before word and entirely within awe. It was a deliberate engagement with another medium of non-mediated expression, and one that hits more faithfully than poetry at the unsaid, at that uncommunicated *aegis* shielding

Being itself. Word plunged into the flesh and pigment of the paint, revisiting it repeatedly throughout the writing. The gaze of the art prevented the poetic act from becoming self-enclosed expression tacitly to an out-there abstracted other. It was the carnality of spirit married to the kind of spirit that leavens flesh.

A handful of Carol's works were in progress, and I witnessed and wrote alongside their inception and completion, from start to finish. Two of the works in the book were my own naked body—Levinas' shivering nudity—reflected and accentuated under glass playing with what is seen and unseen. Carol's choice of my faceless nudity was intentional response to my poetry as gazing upon her creation, re-creating me as self. My poetry re-creating her art, completing the other in the unfolded faces of Being. We are creating and being brought into creation by the other, conjuring a creative fidelity, letting the other enjoin each self to the luminosity of first wisdom, becoming full participants in that wisdom and light, allowing for a heightening and a magnification of experience. Our works placed themselves into the other, placed on the horizon between time and eternity, securing a foretaste of the senses in the resurrected state. This process involved an overflowing of her rhapsodic color and immortalizing image into writing. The final parts of each section of the book have shared poetry to reflect her art anchoring each section of the book.

In this radical and truer philosophy, art and poetry are not picked up and put down, they are not even an extension of one's being, instead they are a foretaste of union in Heaven where senses may cross the divide, where touch of the other communicates sight, and the taste of tears on the cheek speak of the miles of unspoken history. It is a grafting together of ultimate Being as final and ultimate person, hitting at the interior dynamite of the God-Man himself, of Being becoming flesh and blood.

This may be a novel and radical philosophizing, but it is the magnification of medieval epistemology too! It is intentionality lived out in an unabashedly cruciform reality. I am always the other *as other* and that is dramatically heightened when God became man. I must reveal the other, the artist, that I have taken in and become in the act of knowledge. What I have become is the other—that creator or the artist's self she presents to me in this interplay of appearance and reality, the seen and unseen. We are engaged in that *metaxy* that resides between *eros* and *agape*, between the up and the down. What the artist takes in when knowing the *self* is the unity of the illumination of my own self. This is my *poesis* which reveals both the artist's self in progress, and the artist's self whom I have become, when knowledge is, in a way, all things. More still, when I first reveal to the intentional artist her own self, I do so only because my soul knows itself only in the face of otherness, because the artist has revealed my own self, my *poesis* as illuminating her *self* in me. The only origin of this infinitizing mutual dependency would be that each acts from eternity when acting in time. The power and surrender of this infinity is dramatically revealed when God become man.

It is critical that we recognize the unbroken thread in all human experience: any act of thought, engagement, experience places us simultaneously inward—through and beyond ourselves into our originary filiation with the uncreated as mystery at root in all things—and outward—into the other as other of our shared world of incarnality. It is never one or the other, all human experiences place us within this dynamic twofold intentionality which stretches human persons beyond themselves in order to be themselves. No human person is a static entity, a closed essence; the union of body and rational soul, flesh and spiritual tending, allows us *to experience, to be experienced, and to experience being experienced*. To think is to think of things, to be a being of and in the midst of presences, persons, places, relations. This interiorization of the other, which includes the form of self that the other has previously exteriorized, and the exteriorization of the self, which includes a form of the other previously interiorized, evokes the very essence of conversation. This inward and outward process of becoming the other as other is grounded on our participation in God's uncreated To Be, which is epiphanically experienced in us as moving and incarnated images of eternity. This is the intentional or tending structure inherent in all human acts, and it is the path of a real and living Christian philosophy, a philosophizing *in* Christ.

What is a *Christian* philosophy? How can we answer that question if we ignore that Christ poured himself into all the tabernacles in every town and kingdom and city, grafting bodies and souls to his own. This truer philosophizing within this book, this radical *poesis* of art and poetry, reflects this powerhouse demand of the interior reified Transcendental that Christ accomplished when he overcame death. We are never called to be thinkers looking out to an abstracted eternal, we are given a hand in the game of all games. In Christ, we may re-create eternal life through our own dying. We do so through the impossible, through a sharing of our whole being with the other—the poet and the artist—we must pour ourselves through others into Christ who is Other and who *Is*, who is each self dying to live eternally.

A NOTE ON THE BLACK AND WHITE ART

The artist, Carol Scott, rigorously manipulates the boundary of tints and pigments and contrasts their shades and vibrancies in intricate inviting form. Her work in color always involves nuanced unfolding prisms of the unconcealed and concealed presence through a sustained intensification of color. Color crescendos, dips below the waves, swells, impresses upon the eye, overthrows senses, hints at the vast concordial of spirits housed in the divine, which for our eyes appear as the fantastical longed-for *eros* because we cannot experience reality fully, so dimmed with sin and loveless mediocrity, and of the latent acceptance of the long historical patterns of compromising Transcendental salvific Beauty for rote utility. She may capture with rapt exactingness the still-life object, but she does not intend it to be memory art, a mere recitation of the image perceived through the diminished returns of a human life closed to incarnational perception.

Carol is most particularly the striking, innovative colorist who hits the threshold, the supporting lintel, between the mortal confines of beautiful creative imitation and divinely freeing absolute creative action. The latter is reserved for the Divine Artist, and for the rarest of earthly artists; they are gifted, as is Carol, with a grace-infused mind and soul filled in obediential power and potency to God. Her use of color is a listening, an attunement to the music of the heavens, it is formed of the waters at the estuary of all baptism, and it covers canvases with the oils that anoint faces readying for death, not as end, but as beginning. It is not art of snippet and side story, it is not art meant to shock and fade as increasingly irrelevant facet of culture, but of *the* story that resides below our feet and inhabits the air above our heads, and enjoins us all in one flesh through and beyond sight.

After such a detailed description of Carol's use of color, one may wonder why she chose to have her art, so entrenched in the force and eloquence of color, to be in black and white. It should also be noted the risks involved, her medium is color and to relieve her canvases of that dramatic intensity, appears to extinguish air itself, to snatch the wind from the seas and ask the sails to billow and pilot the boats home.

But the ultimate game of all games is in play, *les jeux sont fait*. . . .

Carol sought to invest the book with the visual living mood that the poetic word had tarried along its linguistic thighs as redolence, or had pressed upon its figurative head as violent thorn. She speaks of creating new art from old, as all truth is both older than the oldest bones preserved in blackened peat, and newer than the child born yet this morning. For Carol, to revisit the past is to form something other, and we are remodeling ourselves constantly in the hallways and corridors of time; each possesses a labyrinthian heart, with only so many beats left until the maze, we trust and pray, is lifted.

Carol's work not only transferred impeccably into black in white, it transmuted itself into a dreamscape haunting litany of secret eternal forms. Her canvases, undressed gently into the two primal shades—where the delicacy of balance and power, and mystic revelation originate—became vespers sung in setting sun, and the matins of darkest, coolest morning. In the black and white, her art transposed body, glass, softness of petal into a monastic passage inside every *miseremini mei*. The art recast in black and white recalled Christ's agony in the garden, of our languishing, waiting, altitudinous ecstasy, hoping for sight of the risen Lord when our fingers are dipped into his sides as wells of pigment, ink, blood, tears, light, and shade. Carol's black and white realized, in stirring, indelible form, the singular human soul kneeling in silence before the evocative Other, who beckons us beyond vision.

Fallen Down, by Carol Scott

Foreword

IN ONE OF THE APHORISMS gathered in *The Grain of Wheat,* Hans Urs von Balthasar writes, "Meaning is always richer than interpretation." Which meaning? That of the work of art? Of the world? Of one's own life? Of God? The aphorism appears in a chapter called "Man," suggesting all the above, that this is a foundational truth of the human condition. We are always immersed in more than we can interpret. We ourselves are always more than we can fully figure out. To say that our actions, including our artistic efforts, mean more than we consciously realize is not a testament to irrationality but to the profound richness of being, of our own being, of the artistic image and poetic word.

Balthasar could be a poetic writer, but this aphorism is as abstract as it is pithy. Contrast it with the visceral poetic image that Caitlin Smith Gilson uses to make a similar point in her "Author's Note" on these ten remarkable poetic decades:

> The poet stands at the portico as experience is read *through* her. This is a gate where entrance does not afford exit. At times, it is a low door where the torrent of pressured water is rushing through. As intensively imitative of creation, the poet must remain affixed to each corner of the doorway, taking on what flows relentlessly past her body, and through her appetitive inclination. She is not asked to direct the water.

Smith Gilson is a poet fully alive to the torrent of meaning that always rushes over and through our bodies and their senses, our minds, the depths of our souls. Her eschewal of most punctuation, and especially of end-stopped lines, attests to the inspiring torrent. Hers is a poetry of all the senses, of their synesthetic mixings, of how experience resists our attempts to divide it between the various sense organs. The poem "I Feel More Than I See," co-written with the visual artist Carol Scott, explicitly reflects upon this. To fully appreciate Smith Gilson's poetry, you must speak it aloud, enfleshing it via your own senses, relishing its repetitions and rhymes, its cadences and vigor. The richness of Smith Gilson's poetry enables it to achieve one of the primary aims of art. Preoccupied and anxious, encased in the thick wetsuit of the ego, we all-too-often register the great torrent of life as a sprinkle. The torrent of Smith Gilson's own poetry reinvigorates our senses. As Jennifer Newsome Martin wrote in an illuminating foreword to Smith Gilson's first poetry collection *Tregenna Hill: Altars and Allegories*, her writing "involves (even demands!) the attention of the full sensorium."

If I were to quibble with anything in Smith Gilson's image for how meaning exceeds interpretation, it would be the poet's courageous fixity in the portico, taking in the torrent. In modernity, we have downplayed the receptivity of the artist. This image corrects for that. But it risks overcorrection on its own. For the artist does take up what she receives. She moves, mediates, acts. This side of art receives its due (while also hinting at hubristic temptations) in "The Artisan," another of this collection's poems that Smith Gilson co-wrote with Scott:

> Creation not as God but from God
> Let there be light
> Finding yourself by being yourself
> Other than self
> Original
> Not a copier
> A doer who also dreams
> A maker of things

These poems are not simply the impresses of torrential experience. They are experiences felt, thought, contemplated, dreamed, prayed, synthesized, connected, arranged, crafted. It takes a mighty poetry, a mightily honest poetry, to press on from the impress of experience to the limits of the sayable. Smith Gilson writes such poetry.

Smith Gilson's is a sensual poetry, an incarnational poetry, a sacramental poetry. Transcendence is not somewhere beyond immanence in these poems. It erupts *within* immanence, deepening her experience of the world even as it suggests a depth behind surfaces and far exceeding the senses:

> At final day
> Knee deep in dance
> Legs kicking the water
> Out beyond the garden curve
> To the very myth of you
>
> You have come upon me

> Floating unexpectedly
> Fathomless dream
> I dip my fingers first
> Then my wrist
> Into deep that calls upon deep
> ("Trevignano across the Way")

Still, such encounters with God are never available on demand: "The incommunicable / Opens and closes the garden gate" ("Anguillara"). Our world is the place where God's radiance shines forth in endless variety but also where we feel the desolation of divine distance, of divine absence:

> The floor is smooth and cold
> It reminds of lake and diving well
> Of abundant water spilling from lips
> But I am days without water
> Hanging on your perfumed rose hips
> ("Your Prayer Is Coarse Wood")

We feel this absence not in some dualized ethereal soul but in our ensouled bodies, in the coldness of the floor where we kneel in prayer, in the ache of the back, in the parched lips.

In Smith Gilson's poetry, the experience of overwhelming excess, of superabundance, is always torqued by a sense of frailty, of passing away, of dispersion. To use the archetypal image of myth and scripture and poetry, the blossom soon withers, droops, crumples inward, gives up its petals: "Midnight apparitions of fallen blooms" ("The Untitled"). This tension will be of no surprise to those who have read Smith Gilson's collection *Tregenna Hill* or her profound philosophic-theo-poetic meditations on death in *As It Is In Heaven*. Her poetry is always marked by this paradoxical tension between an ecstatic openness to excess and an ascetic recognition of time-bound finitude: "The never before and never more undress me in their embrace" ("Maundy Thursday"). Watching the sand run through the hourglass can of course unsettle. It can tilt one toward despair:

> But please, please one year all the same
> One more bat squeak of time
> By which the things that are forever yours are mine
> ("The Wager")

Timebound existence means the deterioration, sometimes slow, sometimes rapid, of one's body. It means facing the prospect of one's own death. Like Gabriel Marcel and Emmanuel Levinas (and contra Martin Heidegger), however, Smith Gilson knows that far more devastating is the loss of the other, the separations from friends and family that time inevitably brings, as in "I Surrender to What May Come," and the ultimate separation from them in death, as in "Another Theban Cycle."

We see the tension between excess and finitude too in Carol Scott's striking images that accompany and inspire these poems. The facets of glass, the glint on fish scales, the glow on curtains, the shine of a race car's chrome—all suggest the way things ecstatically refract and augment the radiance of being. In her "Artist's Statement," Smith Gilson encourages us to seek out Scott's artworks in their original resplendence. In this collection, they are presented in monochrome. This stark palette, together with the way that several of Scott's crystal glasses are tipped over, suggests the fragility, the constant pouring out.

The tension between excess and finitude can be lived in several ways. The latter can heighten the former, investing each moment with a sense of preciousness, of *carpe diem* intensity. Living such a way, "Death is dueling partner / Friend not enemy" ("Death Is Not the Enemy," co-written with Scott). The tension can become a dance in the throes of lovemaking, "Playing nonsense and pretense / Playing with death as plaything hurled high" ("Calyx"). Sex, "la petite mort," is one of the primal sites, the primal rites, where this tension is explored, both in life and in this collection.

Smith Gilson suggests that a swashbuckling *carpe diem* approach to life, as alluring as it may be, is not enough. In her profoundly embodied Christianity, the tension between excess and finitude is taken up and consummated in cruciform *kenosis*—a radical taking in of the other and pouring out of the self: "Break me and dip the bread into your blood" ("Maundy Thursday"). The passage of time, the undoing of the self, can become an always more complete opening of oneself to the world, to others, and to God. Only a radical undergoing of finitude thus brings us to the everlasting. The several poems co-written with Scott are often marked by a mischievous wit. In "What Is Your Story?" we are told that the "egg" of the "Ego" must be broken if you want to be "Part of a beautiful hollandaise."

So much Christian art of the past century, even when it seeks to shock, seems tame and abstract alongside the intensely living drama of these lines of poetry. We are gifted here with a mystic's profound, vivid, and strange writings. We should be grateful for this gift, for its vision, wisdom, and challenge, as it stirs us from the numb stupor of this secular age.

Steven E. Knepper
Virginia Military Institute

The Last Laugh, by Carol Scott

Dedication

I CLOSE MY EYES and see the nail in Christ's hand, the painting of you bathing your child, Mother Mary in redolent blue, St. Teresa in Ecstasy by the Murano glass, brilliant cordials on their way, champagne flutes invading time and space with joy, countless progress photos, heartbreaking reflections, light upon light, love with love. Your art tells your life. I thank Our Lady for our friendship, for all the laughter, compassion, and always our Rosary. To my dearest friend Carol, who unveiled the living heart of God—the weeping, abandoning, ravishing Beauty itself—which lives in her.

My friend Caitlin, I have a story to tell of friendship and creativity. Writing poetry came like a strong wind out of the bluest of skies from the oddest place. Caitlin was in Rome, and I was texting photos of my artwork in progress. She was texting poetry. Words were texted with comments that these would make great lines for a poem. Pouring thoughts into thoughts we wrote. I dedicate this to my beloved writing partner, Caitlin Smith Gilson

I think with my eyes
and see with my soul
As you say it
my heart listens
When you speak my lips party (part)
The soles of my feet
Direct my path
We are connected so colorful it hurts my eyes
Like nature seeks the light
Sounds becoming music

—Carol Scott

Acknowledgments

WE WOULD ALSO LIKE TO THANK Cyril O'Regan, William Franke, Matthew Levering, Joseph Terry, D. C. Schindler, Daniel Fitzpatrick, Steven Knepper, and Micheal O'Siadhail for their astute attentiveness, intellectual and spiritual rigor, and care toward this project.

To our dear friend Susan, whose unmatched critique undresses the muses.

To my beloved family, Jim, Tiffany, Daniel, Sarah, Jack, Noah, Alexis, Caroline. You know my love for you all.

Many thanks to the brilliant, engaging, and generous editorial team at Wipf & Stock, particularly Michael Thomson, Matthew Wimer, Jonathan Hill, Mike Surber, EJ Davila, and Zechariah Mickel. We are especially grateful to Robin Parry, our exceptional editor, who has helped transform the book from a labor of love into a work of art.

To my friends at Holy Cross who have helped along the way during the tribulations, you know who you are. I am humbled and grateful to know you.

To Irina, you will always be my sister, the one who taught me the great joy of friendship.

I am entirely grateful for my family. For my dear Fred, you own my heart, I am not worthy of how you have remade it in yours. To my beautiful, intelligent, loving, luminescent daughters, Mary and Lily, I am the luckiest mother in the world. Every day is a gift.

I. THE FIRST DECADE: GOD

"Spirit is never an object; nor a spiritual reality an objective one. In the so-called objective world there's no such nature, thing, or objective reality as spirit. Hence it is easy to deny the reality of spirit. God is spirit because he is not object, because he is subject."

—Nikolai Berdyaev, *Spirit and Reality*

The Fisher of Men, by Carol Scott

MAUNDY THURSDAY

My Lord, I am bathed in blood and sin
As sweetness of song transports age and neglect
Into undelivered ages upon age
Neglect me and do what you will
Ignore every half-spent, misspent thought of mine until I am yours

My Lord I am bathed in your blood and my sin
It soaks my clothes and my hair, chills and tires me, confuses my tears,
rocks me in the cradle, in the heavy down
Lowered into mothering arm held firm in the torrent of sun
Wraps me as the panting deer from the buckshot
Lowered, burst lung, bleeding out
Amid the mud and dung
Muddled and more to soak the ground
So much more reflected on the pavement, on the gravel and stone
Dried on the tongue in the finality to come
Lay down, helpless movement, bereft in un-reflected remorse

Is this it? Is this it, my Lord?
Neck to its side, unresistant as it is broken once more
One more composition redesigned to do your will
Slice my throat
Break my neck
Take your time in mine, hand on chest, ravaged and conquered
Presses and presses of thorns into my eyes

My Love of unacknowledged compassion
My Love of roses overflown
I am without recourse soaked in all blood and sin
Sinless drops of blood anoint the places on my face and chest
Resting on your earth, drowsy and small
The birds round the bay tide and far away hills have come bid me sleep
These vacancies of my fatted heart pull down into singular beats
I tire of your love
Forgive me
I tire of good things

One beat less resistant than the next, each drawn into your languishing misery
You have come before and after me, and through me, beside and below me
You remain in all my nothing of nothing words jumbled and confused

Is this it? Is this it, my Lord?
I conspire in your love
Forgive me
Relieve me
Break me and dip the bread into your blood
My neck is at its side, unresistant and in your care
I place my head upon your earth
Your chest seeps threefold
Your flesh grants space in threes
Your body weeps into me the great night which awaits all unfinished things
Who is it that has come to caress every little hold over hope and walled up innocence behind the wooden door
tucked into its frame
welded into its master lock and key?
The long dressing gown that trails and weaves a thread of clay amid the upturned moonlit earth is soft to touch and weighted with centuries of threefold weeping

My Lord I am clothed in your blood and all sin
The never before and never more undress me in their embrace
Chasing me in their encasement
Hunting me as prey already wounded and bloodied
My scent for the hounds
Pulling my heart down into a single echo, one chamber wall to the next
Volume and percussion
Every ounce of my blood
You take so little of me my Lord

Why do you take so little of me, my lamb of all lambs?
Break me and dip the bread into your blood
In the valley of misunderstanding
I lay betwixt the stars and the past, wondering at last, wondering

Is this it? Is this it, my Lord?

CHRIST'S COMING

Christ
My Christ
Why did you descend so far
Into the place without name?

I have salt on my lips
Caked on each bough
Petrified wood of my mouth
I can't move to motion your name
My flesh is now rock
Nothing
Nothing came

All I need is one drop
One drop of you
One drop of your dying
Unworthy that I am
Unworthy of your opened flesh
Crystal rough comes the sweet sugar
Waiting to melt with you

Numberless wound
It's ripped your heart
Torn its cord
Hung nail
Stretched to dry
Your essence trailing behind you
Death as food
Spread through century
Bewildering me in your perfect love

I can only begin and end with bended knee
If only I knew how to dig myself
Into the night of your first coming
Under you
Through you
But I am not worthy for you
To enter under my roof

Christ
My Christ
My God of Eros and sleep
Abandoned breathtaking shiver
Of your breath upon me
God of winter
God of the wilds
God of the steep
Why was your body so deep into soul
Into the place without name?

I want you to come my God
My God
Come as my death
Trace and entrance me
Sacred resounding necromancy
But I am loaned out
Shipped far away in foreign land
Eden's lost child
Willful pulling of roots with chaffed sides
A crushed and broken leaf of long ago
Buried darkly in grit and snow

God of all gods
My Christ
I want you to come as my life
Come upon me as water
Holy Ghost of the heavenly host
Down my back
Down into the forest of the last post
Last call
Last resort
You confuse love and death
Loved to death
Lost and winding down
Found in you

You remain inside me
Till earth turned to ice
At the center of all mystery

Thrice graced hand upon my chest
Upon our hearts
You, the great alone
Salvaging hope
From bruised cornerstone

Christ
My Christ
All love comes
All love comes through you

THE FALCONER

"Lord, I am not worthy that you should enter under my roof, but only say the word and my soul shall be healed."

The falconer
Glissading into muscled physicality
Devastates with motiveless lips
A hieroglyph of ancient sex
Electra binding Oedipus
Blinders blinding context
All language born from his inner grip
Impeccable distending falconry
Scanning the lay of the land

Tear me to pieces
Dissever me in elected atonement
I am stumbling in my insides
Fallen to the floor
Running from Godhead
Far below the covered door

Perfect wicked grace
Detestable grace
Mouthing my name
Intractable riddling hand
Scanning
The lay down lay of land

Send your bird of prey
With tanned corset
Firm around the face
Absolve me
Cover its eyes
This savage blessing
Covering my eyes

The falcon
Moves along intrinsic lust
Gliding
Sanding the sky
Particulate wood
Matter ripped to shreds

The Rood
Bearing down
It is bearing down
Devastating bitter grace
Wiping the floor
Prying the lids from my eyes
Once more

VENI DONUM

Dear God, fool of all fools, lover of all loves
Shall I die in spring with the freshness of honeysuckle on my tongue?
Will you make a wreath of herbs which trails its scent through lawn and home?
Rosemary and forest and oceans of salt that sticks to lips after long swims home

Of home
Of home and kin
Indistinct happy chatter wafting as pots boil down halls
Upstairs, beds, rooms, and lives

Of home
Of wood and doors and light and beams
Of sinless ambiance and quieted down covers
Windows which stream light from rafted ceilings
Nights cooled into the eternal quiet where each step records its own shuffled sound

Your love terrorizes me
It confuses earth and sky
It plays with the line down my back
Separate me into two and make me one
Come home my love, my fool, my God

Of home
Of long swims home
Of fields becoming rivers
Of kisses overflowing into water
One arm reaching towards the next in motion under the moon
Without end you promised
Without end

Of homes without end
The hermit crab scurries from one shell to the next
The tide is low my love, my fool of all fools
My God of gods

THY WILL BE DONE

Thy Will be done
It means that I will love you
And do nothing but love you
To the end of timekeeper's
Last wave of hand
Dot of sand
Drop of dew

You knew all along
How much love can do
How it rips the sail in two
You cannot move away
The wind will not obey your broken sail
Now the winding sheet upon Christ's face
Graceless ruins
In my undying love

Thy Will be done
It means that I will love you
And do nothing but love you
Shot through the cracked vase
Into the very scope of the rifle
To the eye which looks ahead
But knows not how to feel

You knew all along
Beyond the shot which has struck
Through you to me
Wounded me inside you
Tethering us indelibly
That I would love you beyond end
Surpassing your fear
My love remains your great friend
My undying Will be done

Thy Will be done
It means that I will love you

And do nothing but love you
Under every sun
In every universe now and to come

My child of sand
Cracked vase
Wound and sun
Thy Will be done

Thy Will be done will devastate you
It will squander what is left of you

Thy Will be done
Will dwindle you to nothing
The dirt of riverbend
All for love
It will cause your lips to part
Cracked and parched
All for love

Love devastates
Decapitates the lesser
The lie
The false head which directs you
You cannot see
You have not the eye

Let me give you love beyond end
Into the mist of the great forgetting
My Will be done

THE LONGIOR VIA

We have a long way to go
Where river and tide cannot abide
What a long descent
One single spent hair split
Shining, frail
Sent to the fire
Lifeless and then dust

All that is
Every lust
Worn-down bed and windowsill
A blown trail of unkempt embers
Drying in the uneven day
Mottled colors none which may stay
None which outlast the stage setting of your play

What a long way between here and there
Into the forest of Passiontide
As lashes which thrust and drive
Pensively
The single emblematic tear
Forged before the fire
Thrown
The wood logs writhe and crack
The bribe of bone into ash

How long has it been?
How long is it now?
A depth of ignorance hems its sighs down my back

Ground my grained heart
Wordless cries sweep the chaff

How long has it been since "once was"?
How long has flesh mingled with blood?

Who knows my Lord of night and cold
Silence and star
Sea and moon
The ramparts upon ramparts have been re-made in you

THE UNTITLED

Midnight apparitions of fallen blooms
Stroking the flames
Place their elective compassion upon my sight

I see how little love is loved
How little I am
And how very small one to another is in the beginning and the end
Forgiven and forgotten

The blush touch and dance aimlessly overflow
As gardens are left to the wild
Some secrets entreat of home before earth
Kiss before shelter
Pure and without need
Given in the purity without need

A misted pink and white separating from the green leaf
Floats down upon my hand
Pulled away from its root by gravity
Your mystery dances through me as blood and wine
All things fall asleep

All things make their way to the stones
Slick with rain
All promises concede
Words relieved

Time knows no place to lay its weight
Tonight, it bowed its unseen face
To the divinity playing along the canopy

Distress my features wide across fields of grain
The winnowing and the scythe
You've placed my perishing heart among the wheat to be gathered
Ground down, and made for bread
My center to be leavened in God's own hand
To be leavened in the blood of the Lamb

Upon the hill of Three
All promises concede
All things fall asleep
Time knows no place to lay its weight
Its hair now pulled back from featureless face
Only say the word
Make the sign and I shall be healed as flowers, as grain, as time regained
Forgotten in time

THE INTERROGATIVE

To the dear undying God of death and dream
A prayer of concealment
Stilled into earthly hour
Tilled ancient forest torn and tossed to the fire

Silent ream upon ream of paper falling to the floor
Pages after you
Unremarked sheet of unkempt time
Line your majestic carnival
Hall of mirrors and sleight of hand
I pick your card
Nothing other than you

How very long have I been yours?
Brought to heel in the exodus land?

Your deck is loaded
Your prayer to unclothe me to the bone
Loaned out one by one
Into the silence redesigned to address your case
Against every plead
You've taken me to the depths of earthly end and deed

Diseased hope upon hope lay down your hope

A prayer of silence to trespass wit
Chides and twists as riverbend
You come in light white linen
Laced and wounded shroud
Cover my face
Long haunting wordlessness
Poured into smoke

Diseased hope upon hope lay down your hope

A silence as old as greed
A silence as old as greed

Has come over me
I prepare the banquet which never was
Nor will be
A silence as old as greed
Has come over me

God: The Shared Poetry of Artist Carol Scott and Caitlin Smith Gilson

Unstoppable, by Carol Scott

REQUIEM

If you dip your finger
Into the blood of my paint
And further your reach
Behind my heart
Then you would know with inborn light
The slower requiem
The Platonic Form
Hothouse strawberries
Overworking the vine

Dip your finger into the wine
Into the wilderness of God's leaving
Departing leaves from winter's tree

If you would dip my finger
Within the paint of your heart
Beyond all Philosophy
Then I would know every sense
Sight overworking the vine
Un-gelded artifices of beauty
Effortless roiling time

Artisan of unspent surrender
Places change beauty
Hemlocked lips
Death will know everyone

No more philosophical meanderings
Into the dark
As light of God
Door opening
Door closing
Run wild
Passions shot
Death will know everyone

DREAMLAND

Sleep is for dreaming
Carnivals of color
Dusky hills
Sunsetting mellow kiss
Little houses of brick and stone
God's own bliss

Night of sleep
Magical lonely wilderness
Dreamland of moonlit froth
Mountainous greenery for orphans and elves
Icy streams into the estuary of dreams
Separated from clay
Shadowy blanketed waters
Asleep on rocking boat

When I let go of my waking world
Color surrounds me
Astounds
The stars debate the night and day
Vanquished monsters
Rollercoasters
Lovers and children
Visions of friends and foe

Above and beyond the ground
Touched and guided
The past is current and moving on
Flown and run
Never wanting to wake
Daybreak could not wait
Some things can only be seen in dreams
Only done in dreams
Thank God
Sleep is for dreaming

GLORY

Glory
In spite all the trouble
God is giving us a gift
Something new to take the place
Of what came before

Toss my faith in your tincture
In your painter's dust
Mixed into oil
A new substance
A believing that can walk into fire
Cross oceans of sand

Make me
The color of leaves changing on the vine
Of fruit picked too late
Too plush
Too perfect
That it calls to mind childhood innocence
A wine the color of straw
Readied brimming joyous innocence
Laughter that knows only the now

Make me believe in beauty that can save
Salvage lost life
Beauty that redeems the soul
Beauty that knows all untold story
Held below the surface of you

Glory
In spite all the trouble
God is giving us a gift
Something new to take the place
Of what came before

SACRED GEOMETRY

Lines

Line that moves to infinity
Line that caresses a form
Lines that are broken
Lines that are boundaries
Lines and more lines and more lines and more lines

Standing in line
Breaking in line
Forming a line

Stepping over the line
The line has been crossed

Forms

Form at the waking bed
Form underneath meaning
Form unsaid
Form held
Form sharp

Forms soft and muscled
Forms angular and gentle as night

Form folded into code
Form explosive
Form shorn and swift

Form smoothing lines, these lines, all lines
Your form in time, preceding time, defeating time

Boxed

Lines becoming a square
Squares becoming a form

Are you in or out of the box?
Square or cool?

Unwrapped

One or two movements
Separate the thick entwined ribbons
Dropping off the box
Discarded to the floor
What have lines made?
What form is in store?

Is it a gift?

II. THE SECOND DECADE: SEX

"Love is what is most terrible and tragic in the world. Love is the child of deceit and the parent of disenchantment, love is the consolation in disconsolateness. Love furiously seeks through its object something that lies beyond it and, not finding it, despairs. . . . In love we seek to perpetuate ourselves on Earth only on the condition that we die, that we surrender our lives to others. The humblest little animals, the lowest living beings, multiply by dividing, splitting in two, ceasing to be the singles they once were. And every act of engendering is a ceasing to be what once was, a splitting, a partial death. Perhaps the supreme delight of engendering is nothing but a taste of death in advance, the rending of one's own vital essence . . . because only in others can we become eternal. There is, without a doubt, something tragically corrosive in the depth of love in its primitive, animal form, in the unconquerable instinct that impels a man and a woman to mix their bodies in furious embrace."

—Miguel de Unamuno, The Treatise on the Love of God

Sweet Treat, **by Carol Scott**

THE JACKAL

The jackal and the lamb have come to dance
Limping and panting
In the curve and dive
Shaking in the standstill complied
Negotiated, fallen inside, fabrics chide
Historic movements in unelected aching thighs
Last things lay exaggerated and hidden
And time is too near

You transfix my silhouette into flesh
You contemplate my face with your sex
You hold my hair and condemn me to rest
You whose fingers lay half suspended between my lips
Held over you I am
I am
And we are
Still now
Still time is too near, close the door
Half permit me into ecstasy

Among the last things that never last
Burn me
Bribe me
Circle me
Take me down
Strip my flesh
But time is too near
To the bones, take them
To the bones then
My jackal with curling stares
Undreamt and rounded down
Time is too near

GLI AMANTI

Drown me in your liquor
Sharpened fermented plum
Steamed in tea

This perfumery of word
Overpowers every earth and star
Falling in cloth

You have undressed my words
With matchless dying
One fingered loop
And you have taken the ornamental robe
Fallen off each shoulder
Down my waist
Dropped to my legs in a well of paint
And your tea steeping elegantly
In the next room

Indefectible, knelt
Stilled and shivered
Arms wasting away into the other
Smooth as moonlit cream
Stirred in sugar

Saturated walls of your dense color
Electrified sliced ginger
Thinner cuts held over the water's heat
My face rubbed in and out of yours
In the steam

My sex is laid out on the table
Madly and wildly
Untameably in love with you
So put me down

All force and tenderness
Most come home to rest

Crystallized light
Pure redolence put to bed
Put me down

I lay in the land outside Tangier
All ocean and desert
Blue and white
Wet and dry for miles beyond sight
The ginger on my lips
Stings of you

DIONYSIUS IN TIME AND SPACE

If the river were any higher
I would lose myself
This is not about swimming
Or laying inside a current
Till transport to the next place

It is that you are the particular
Missed in morning
Hunter's kiss
First and last dream
Bound and unbound wrist
You remade my silhouetted soul in your shade

I can feel your silk
At the end of ever-flowing time

Cooled in weighted sheet
Bested with one ounce of unsourced heat
You make me fall, float, and sink

You undermine the impossible
With nonchalance
The shimmering shivering sex of gods
Bathed in fragrant waterfalls
Skinned fruit on my lips
Rhythm and repurposed word

I can feel your silk
At the end of ever-flowing time

If I go deeper will I breathe?
If I enter this current will I survive you?
The delighting Dionysian death of gods
Love beyond love beyond life
You are these things
These powers and principalities
This particular hour un-passed

You are the exit and the light
I am electrified
Have I already died?

I can feel your silk
Wrapping me
At the end of ever-flowing time

THE WRIT

Your lips sucker-punched in sex
Down me
Take me to the pit

Wrap their ineluctable charm into each of my senses
Wounded in the war of your elected ecstasy
Wound tighter around my waist
Wired shut and opened at will

Every heterodox move traced up my thigh
Into the writ and riot of shared sky
Saccharine sweet and bitter moves

Every command and plea renewed
Drafted on your face
Your sweet face
Against the wall and floor
Round the bend once more
Taken by you
Always by you
My lover of foolish things

LA PETITE MORT

You placed your perfect finger
On my waistband
Faultless
Drawing me into ancient captivity
Your consummate touch
Upon the rim of the glass
Flawless
Diluting my kiss with vineyard wine

Your absolute
Palmed and fingered upon my face
Seas of tears
Untouched as virgin snow

The beekeeper's ecstasy
Pricked lips and contemplative hum
Olives rolled as ice on tongue
Regaining your mastery
Caprice mouthed in winding word
A thicket of scents and nonsense
To know the vowels
The articles stringing together your reason
Easy to part

Your absolute
Palmed and fingered upon my face
Seas of tears
Untouched as virgin snow

The inveterate gamble
Tall as pine trees dressed in snow
Disquieted in the forest of your night

Your absolute
Palmed and fingered upon my face
Seas of tears
Untouched as virgin snow

EL DAMASCO

Heated spells and apricots drowned into readiness by sun
Rolled about in your palm
Oozing their pits into the press
Into the rounded fleshy pushed-in seam

Pulled apart in dreamlike mouth
Time unpassed
Placated by breeze and lean cotton sheet
Culled into shape
Legs bent, stretched to be bent
Bent around your stars and lake
Blood among the roses, bedspread, and board
The deeper give and take

Your head, your face
Your hair toying with your face
Ravished into the slowed down newness of halted form
Stare down the abyss
The kiss unbound

Icarus warmed to touch
Feverish
Bruised by rain
Sugared with raptured painted breast
Cusp of pink and cream

The wail of long untrained sound
That dips to the ground
That hits lower than earth
Dip your finger
Dragged along the ridge of my boxed voice
Bones as hollow as birds
Riding my thigh
Winsome little cry

Moving death transgressing divide
Seducing the covers to the floor

Salting the fruit
Breached stone

We are mangled trees
Low-slung plucked life laying at its side
Crept together and hushed into form

MY SWEAT FROM THE DAY OF YOU

My sweat from the day of you
Has finally come
It closes my eyes
And mimics tears
The waters barely move
Dancing, dividing in two

Throw the pebbles in the water
Seducing the unmoved ground
Displaced as I swim
Separated in the cooled down body blue
Cratering vast lake of you

Watch me come
In your sweat
As water
As sugar water on tongue
A hummingbird upon you
Finely put down
Dropping into the pillow
Skirting nectar
From plum

Too cool is the evening
Crisp air entombing the cobblestone streets
Knitted sweaters
Shivering without fireplace

Too cold a night to bring me to sweat
But try
Pull the wool over my eye
One by one
Thighs exiled from the heavy down
Then descend into fire
Unrepentant
I come
Once again
For you

THE IN-BETWEEN

Chilled silken faces beneath the archway in bloom
Flatter the painted tiles
Blend into the void of night and space
Each star has taken your place
You lace your fingers around my hips
Terracotta crowned into color, twists of lilac and rose
A dust rubbed into oil fingers an inscape of my face
Rolled around in your hands, disfigures every grace

You draw out my flesh with your thumb
Bitten down into earthbound things now mute and dumb
Wrap me into every little square
Turn my neck into your chest
Taper my legs, arms, and breast
To the tiles

Into memory immaculate in line and row
An architect of sky unfound and grounded down
Gasping and gaping, forsaking
You are the heavy geometry weaving through my body
Haunting and hollowing
Placing and turning my shape into yours
Perfect tiles
To the tiles

Alleviate me of your weight
Blown flowers, shaking in the shower
A confused snowfall
Falling one by one in your sweat

I LEFT MY EYES AT YOUR DOOR

I left my gaze at your door
Having forgotten that it is mine

When you find it
Place it in velvet
Navy and all softness
Pull the string
To keep it close

Un-petaled iris
On the bedside table
With your pretty little things
Your study of me

I lost my voice
Speechless upon your lip
Where the pearl sinks
You stained my word
In pinewood scented forest
But I need not speak

All your pretty little things
Gilded rings
Perfumery
Half spent drink
Melted obscenely into warmth
Your study of me

My lips are numbed with ice
They can live apart from my face
Soon they may rest
Next to my gaze
Remade in the velvet crush
In your pretty little jewelry box
Your study of me

Sex: The Shared Poetry of Artist Carol Scott and Caitlin Smith Gilson

Pure Life, by Carol Scott

SEXY WILL OUT

You may blush my hills
In every way
In pillow kisses

Feed me your lines
Interlaced in afternoon light
In pillow talk

Sexy will out

The human figure
Intertwined
In wilderness of violets
You unsexed me in the sheets

Sexy will out

The nectar of angels
Bondage gift
Earthbound
In pillow rapture

STONE FRUIT

Stone fruits
Find their way
Ripened
Tongue in cheek
By glorious hand
At its peak
Mountainous ascent
Twirling heights
Parachute imperiously released
Floating down in a blanket of blush

In velveted mauves and sunset straw
Crescendo of blackberries
Squeezed in thumb
In your midday maddening breeze
Purpled globes of pulp
Brushless, bridled, and unbruised
Magnificently daring
In and out of scope

All in room with ceiling high
Shafts of light
Nimble fingers play, slay, and captivate
Thrown seeds for birds to feed
Tongue in cheek
Etch the orchard of body and birth
Whose tongue and whose cheek?

All in room with ceiling high
Voyeuristic moments of celebrated joy
With naked feet and bended knee
Transcendent moments of memory
Bold and looked upon by choice
Without shame
Light rocks the body firm

Devastating the norm
Hint of shoulder bare
Waging design from thinnest air
Moving through thunder
With flowing hair
The owner of pulse
Raised and dropped
Ever steadied
Keeper of lightning
Framer of perfection
Ruler of writ
Fruit sucked to its pit
Without shame
Light rocks the body firm

SEDUCED BY THE SOUND OF YOU

Your voice
Spun silkworm
Threaded, lingering
Downed rubies
Only the hint of sting

Called by the word of you

Your voice alone
Could make me come
With you
Far away

Beckoned by hearing you

Your voice condensed
Squeezed between my legs
Pouring in and out of me

Calling your name
Between breathing

Your voice is deluge
Flooded plains
Your every word
Rolling barrels
Rotating around an unfixed axis

Sensing the voice of you

Your word at the bedroom door
Unfastened clasp
Dropped gown
Casks of sugarcane liquor
Your last syllable
Resting on my tongue

Speaking between sighing
I hear the music of you

EXPERIENCE

I could come, come with your kissing . . .
I surrender
When I look at you
I see you naked
God
I love you more than life

III. THE THIRD DECADE: SURRENDER

"Oh, we shall convince them that only in surrendering their freedom to us and submitting to us can they be free. Well, shall we be right or shall we be lying? They will see for themselves that we are right, for they will remember to what horrors of slavery and confusion Your freedom led them. Freedom, science, and independence of spirit will lead them into such a labyrinth and confront them with such miracles and such insoluble mysteries that some of them, intractable and savage, will destroy themselves, while others, intractable but less strong, will destroy one another; and those who remain, feeble and unhappy, will crawl up to our feet and will cry out to us, 'Yes, you were right, you alone held his secret, and we are returning to you: save us from ourselves."

—Fyodor Dostoevsky, *The Brothers Karamazov*

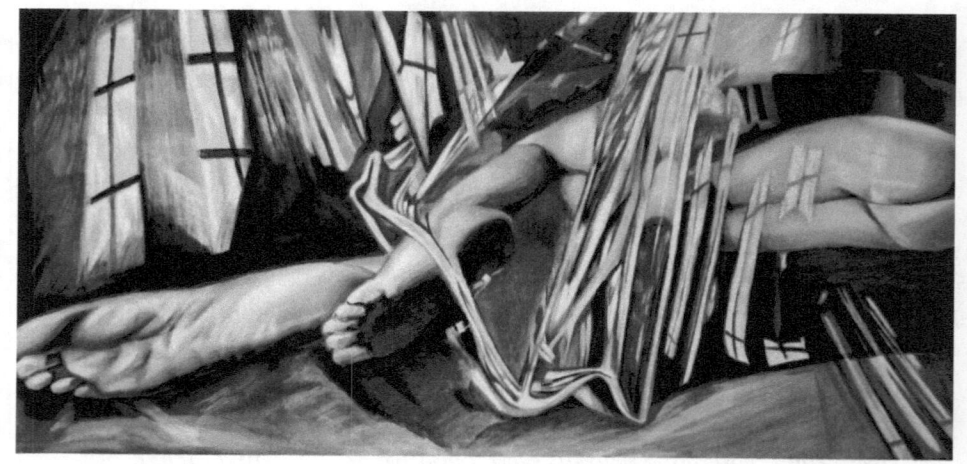

St. Teresa in Ecstasy, by Carol Scott

IL LADRO

You robbed the color from my cheeks, tenderly floating down in the trace of tears
The palest color, tasting of oceans and time
Wildflowers, honey, and honeysuckle
The Nordic spring air recollects the color from my face
Pale lilies beside the waterfall
Bone white petals
Suffer not from care

A novena to the past outpaced the raw cut stems
Cracked opened chests
Come now
Come home to your heart
Cut down, fold and pressed into your book
One long spectacle flowing from your eyeline into mine
Past my sight
Down my thighs
Drown the petals with force
You robbed the sound from my voice
Holding you
Pressing through you
One sigh became yours
Consigning your newness to my face
Your age un-erased

We are
Drafted lines with charcoal and shade
We are
Comprised immortality renting out time
We are
A honey-colored humility paying down the heavy fine

The thief in the night with my sweetness on his lips
Took my heart into his dance
The thief in the night
Took me to his stillness
Intrudes my memory

Into still memory
The picture beside the bed
Beside the unmade bed
Beside the grave filled with earth and death
The thief in the night robbing the color from my cheeks
Kisses me as he goes

CHAVAH

She wept a reordered world into Being
A forgotten god at the edge of existence
Grafting time and space to her body
Through her body to mine

Legs in and out of shadow writhing in wintry spells
One fulcrum of tear weighted from within
Weighted and falling the drowsy distance from her cheek
Down her muted breast
Curving the soft mound
Twirling below into her heated absence
Red and pink
Wetted tongues forked and joined
Dancing and executing the other
Paced and panted exotic silence
Pushed in and out the rhythmic lance of death and love
One single sound precedes thy will be done

Hips thrust through shade and sweat
Her sex dotting the flowers
Touching the orchids
Making carnivals of pain pandering every bend of my body
Torn and shredded as paper into yours
Forever remade by your unending decomposition

The pith of your lips sucked apart in mine
Perilous confidence
Perjurious substance
From here in your heart
To there in exile

Suns ever setting behind me
Too warm and too cold
Too much and too little
All too little and never enough forgiveness

Of nights cooler and uncompassionate on my skin
In my flesh and bones
Brittle thinning bones
Your taste on my lips left dried and parched

Blood of my blood
Life of my life
Puckered and pulled into form
Inside
Outside
Pulsing with the folded flesh of your perfume
Draped into me
None other than me

Blood of my blood
Life of my life
I weep a world of discontented *eros* drawn as moths to flame

Far beyond the garden gate
She laid me down spread apart into every tide
The floral canopy of the bridegroom left in wait
Hedgerow of broken innocence invited into lowly passion
And last things alone are condemned to last

THE ARMORY

Your exquisite armory
With one deadly weapon
One entangled gaze
Contouring the angles of my waist
To Adam's rib
Pull back the covers

The brick swift heave and plunder
You have taken me down
Cut in half
Arrow and bow with rapt precision
The whirl of the shaft lower than eye and ear
I stand but have no knees, no feet
My breath made weak
Diabolical honeydew sugared reverence
Pull back the covers

A singular moan
conspicuous collarbone traced and toned
Hollowed corridors
Ancient stone
My breath made weak
Angelic tongues to brackish boundary
Languishing deer lapping streams
So long ago and many year
Pull back the covers

All the nettles descending
Pressed firm in your book of night
Your secret sorcery upon the magnolia
Your scent entering the knotted wound
Permeating the gape
Spilling my substance
Upon the reified thing
Pull back the covers

Arching our spines as fallen blades of grass
One death-defying godsend
The spirit casts wide upon water and wine
Breaching the air meters below heaven
Pull back the covers

Twilight of gods descend the mountain
You double as unrecorded depth
Throwing me down in silk and gold
Pull back the covers

Every orbiting star becomes flesh and descends the high wall
Passing over the standing guards
Into the secretive court
Cherished one who makes fear and love
Pull back the covers

Your armory is more precious than woven silk and spun gold
Pull back the covers

Every orbiting star of mine has fallen down
Where are your hands when flesh must fall
Must fall as stars?
More precious than silk and gold
Pull back the covers

SURRENDER IN SPADES

If you are going to take hold
Make sure you take it all
You can defeat me with a look
I'll never have the upper hand

You have me riding bands of sky
I am falling faster than I can fly

You can trespass me
Play me
Topple my house of cards
I fold at the sight of you
I'll never have the upper hand

You have me riding bands of sky
I am falling faster than I can fly

Take every card from every deck
I am playing without power
I have nothing to shuffle, stack, or draw
Emptied suits
Waiting for you
I'll never want the upper hand

You have me riding bands of sky
I am falling faster than I can fly

If you are going to break my game
Take my sound
Create my term
Rock my body firm
Make sure I dip all the way down

You are
Dear God
You are
What I lost before life

CHRIST'S KISS

Dearest Christ
Will you take me
As pieces of your body
Somewhere between heaven and hell

I want your kiss on my lips
I cannot understand anything else
I lost my taste for words
I need your kiss
Your Word made flesh

If only I could survive your love
If only I knew you well enough
Between these nails
Then I would survive your mercy
Your felt kiss on my feet to my lips
In rain

If only I knew you when I was dead
If only I claimed your kiss cold in my grave
If only I knew you as I know my face

I do not want to survive you
I lost my taste for words
I am losing my touch as the rain falls
If only I knew you coming upon the wave

Press your face upon mine
Somewhere between these nails
If only I had touched you
If only I knew how to die with you
I cannot feel your life upon the water

Rain falls upon the Cross
And all your blood is washed away
Beneath your feet

I want to cup the arches of your feet
Lick the iron of each nail
Drink your wine
All your blood has washed away
Below the floorboards

If only I knew you well
If only I knew your touch
Rain-washed Cross
Of Spring

How will I know you when I die
I am on the boards
Waiting for you
Let me drink with rain on my lips
Your mercy as a kiss

The salt has lost its savor
I only want your sweetness
Your softest surest kiss
I lay down for you
Rain upon the lamb of the Cross

My Savior
Will you take me as pieces of your body
Inside your heaven
Will you let my flesh be kissed with yours
Will you let my body be made of you

Be a crown of softened thorn
Pushed into my breast
Breathing your elated pain
Tasting of you
Drinking your wine
Until I die

Will you hold me within the earths
Conquered with your kiss
Upon the rain
Between these nails
Will you take me into your tomb

Make me new
Roll the stone
Let me sleep the night of nights with you

RENDERING

Render me timid
Shrouded by softened features
Subdued in your pastel collection
Untouched by sanguine tint

Render me your hollowed bed
Windows of you upon my caress
Miles of yellow and sunlit pink
Strides across the sky, through the clouds
Your fading mauve into whispered bridal white
Chrysanthemum hedges folding over
Drowsy on the stem
Foundlings pulled away

Render me the received
Masses of your silken trace
Into thicketed camouflage
Fresh vanilla shaved into cream
Downing me in your perfumery
Artery of ecstasy
Bended rain-soaked knee

Render me your sweetest sex
Touching the drawn edge of my little breast
Rounding me into firmness
Rose wine blushed into alabaster curve
Softened belly pressed in your hand
Sup of fleece and chrysalis husk
Underworked in the aching land of dream
Pulling gently into your glacier lake

Render me a fragmented pot
Nothing contained
Everything seeping to the floor
Sheltering you in my collapse
All that I am
In steep embankment

EBB TIDE

I shall conform
Thrust from the stem
Insignificant Icarus in revolt
Breaches the furthest reach of the water's edge

I shall conform
Your cavernous will enamored
Trapped in netted longing
Reigning in the ebb tide
With pulse and threat

I shall conform
The air in still waiting
Encircles the large breath which chills the skin
Laying its eternal dying upon my shoulders and neck

I shall conform
The moon's perverse promise
It cannot guide
Bare and unknowing

I shall conform
Do you not see the immemorial figure behind the silkscreen,
Hushing me in absence, bathing me in its silent stage?

How shall I conform without your word?
How shall I be without your face upon my chest?

You have taken every last cast-aside breath that I can give
I have no more to conform but this—
The word that lays upon my tongue and remakes me in my sleep
I shall go there, to the place beyond place and rest in your arms

YOUR TERESA IN ECSTASY

Un-leaven the bread
Settle in
Fade out
Raise the dead

Slip in with roughness complied
Chide the hairs on my back to stand
To strain for your glassed attention
Threaded as innumerable strand
Your presence consecrates the room
Deconsecrates the chapel
Riding high at my tightened thigh

The furnishings imitate your shape
The windows heave and drape
The patina rough as bark
Not even flooded Tiber
Has power of death to save me

The fire is not hot enough in hell
It is not hot enough
To release me from this ecstasy

Furnaces frame your face
Voices falling as sheathes of gold
Dip down ordered fantasy
Dripping from gleaming teeth
Theatrical shake of metaled hues
Thunder in the blue

The executor of sex
Embroidering mystery
The darning needles twitch
Pushing and plotting through the wool
Little Teresa with open mouth

Forsaking miles
The emperor of lexicons
Rendering eternity un-atoned
Little Teresa with the upturned sky

The fire is not hot enough in hell
It is not hot enough
To release me from this ecstasy

TODAY IS THE LAST DAY

Today is the last day
I will ever make love to you
You'll be panting between my legs
Lucid in your madness

Today is the last day
You will know who I am
You'll consume me
Till every ocean is red
Till the room
And the covers
And the bed
Are tighter
Than clutched head
At the last bend
Before you fall

When we separate
And our bodies come to their own
And your soul buries down
Into the cleft of my un-breathing lips
In some corner of your world
You will wish you were never born

This is not play-acted faith
Nor brittle desire
In some corner of the world
Every day is the last day of our life

Every engine is dying down
Cellars under cellars of wisdom
Lost and rarely found
The only true love is unrequited

To love perfectly
Is to endure space and silence
Until we cannot be anything else but love

Upon love
Collecting springs of love

This is not play acted faith
Nor brittle desire
I want you to love me perfectly
To be stretched half dead
More alive

Everyday we will love the other till we die
We will wish we were always born
Always new
In every corner of the world
I will belong to you

BEND MY HEART AROUND YOUR WAIST

Bend my heart around your waist
Sun salted snowdrop
Your desire
Anchors my soul
Melting me

What else can I do
In the touch of you?
Perfected crisscrossed Rubicon

I was weighted in the sadness of change
But you came as quickening
All whirling scent
And you had
And you have
And you will have me
What else could I do
Inside the touch of you?

Bend my heart around your waist
Sipped singed lemon peel
All passion
All pain
All action
Bedding my heart
Anchoring my soul

Lay your body on me
On the rink
Condensing ice
Soaked up sorrow
Odysseus on the brink
Shipwrecked pink on pink
Wet from the day of you

Dipped in gold
Edges of indigo

You are the felt knowing
Of my sliding soul

My body ached in sorrow
Weighted dressing gown
But you came to me
You bent your heart around my waist
You are the fatal lines of my hand
On your face
The wax
The warmed sex

Bed of my heart
Anchor of my soul

YOUR SURRENDER

Your surrender that night
It will live with me past forgetting

These are simple words
As you would have it

Some surrenders
Tear up the earth
Bigger than countries

Some surrenders
Are more than heartbreak
More than joy

I am not worthy of your love
More than all oceans
That I have lived
And swum in silence
God and my body interlocked
The sound of the water
My arms carried in my breathing
I cannot translate this to you
This love of open waters and sun
Your surrender will live with me
Past forgetting

These are simple words
As you would have it

Your surrender will live with me
In my lonely dying
In the last ocean I swim
Silently to its shore
The shore that you
I pray
Already know

All dying must touch the alone
More than touch
More than cut tears
Flowing across your face as diamonds

All words of all time
Are the felt mystery of you
Your surrender
It will live with me past forgetting

Surrender: The Shared Poetry of Artist
Carol Scott and Caitlin Smith Gilson

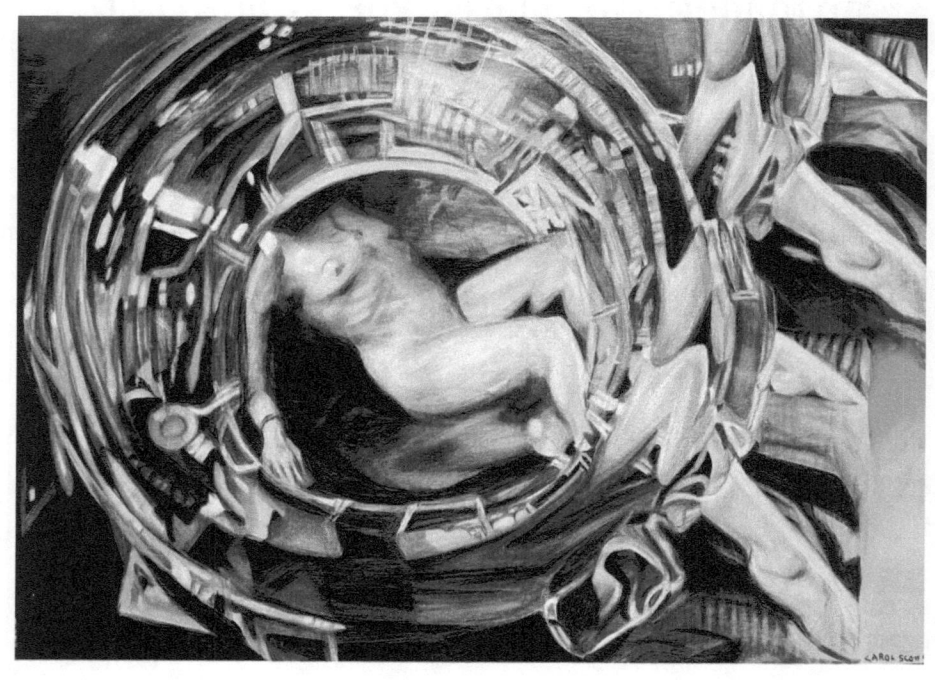

Redolent Blue, by Carol Scott

LIQUID FEELING

Liquid soft surrender
Delicious
Tastes of mangos overripe
Baking in sun

The eye of heaven
Has its own tears
Each sinks into canvased snow
As crystal droplets
No earth below

Gazing cuts of glass
Neither future nor past
Pure palpated presence
Delirious living elixir
Plummeting diamond droplet of pulp
For lucid tongue

Midnight fig assuaged of skin
Immaculate shades of purple
Bewitching blues and yellow
Immortal confectionary
Sweet sponges of cake
Preserved pressed grape
Rioting reds
Madness and wine
Delicious liquid soft surrender
Entwined

Lunacy forced
Power magnified
Magical illusions
Rocking color
Redolent blues
Nothing faded
Full deep
Deepening

Shallowing all light
Liquid feeling of delicious surrender

Spotting, slotting, cocking the palette
Sight imbibed

The brimming aperitif
Bright clean body line
Shaken, stirred, braced
Colors lowering
Hands to waist
Silk stocking sexiness
Rosewood tree rings
Beams of gothic red
Stressing the scene

Godless light
Liquid shards
Sleight of hand
Stabs of delight
Controlled blade of steel
Surrendering
Heaven's might

IN-TIMACY

How beautiful the foot
How graceful the ankle
Knee function without pain
Thighs that were meant to be parted

Beautiful foot graceful
Ankle
Thighs

That were meant to be parted

IN-timacy

I plan to do this till I die

To be with things that are meant to be parted
Most grateful
Gracious thighs
Silken calves
Back of knee

IN-timacy

Delicate stemmed lilies
In the valley of your calves and feet
Loving pain
Hips shivering in slow drifting rain

Beautiful foot graceful
Most grateful
Sweet lingering parting

I plan to do this till I die

I SURRENDER TO WHAT MAY COME

It was never supposed to be this way
What's been taken away
I am to be happy
You are to be my friend

Intentions towards goodness
kindness, fellowship, and fun
I always talk
Wait till you meet my friend

Do not cut us
Dissecting every word and movement
Confronted by your pain

I surrender to what may come

The headlights keep blinding you
The unspoken bitterness
Binding us to silence
To fate that may separate us

I feel your surrounding sorrow
Of self closed inside self
Cocooned in misery
Layered regret
Of past revisited but unlived again

I know you better than you
I already know
Where you do not permit me to go

I cannot tread down this road
But I can love you
And wish you much happiness
Embraces of goodness and peace
Every day I pray
For you

I surrender to what may come

My heart is full
How can you not realize
This time spent together
This decade made of months
Made of afternoons on my sofa
Hours of laughter in every room
How it has meant everything

How can you not understand
No person is replaced by another
You do not need to send yourself away
Every day I pray
For you

Why can't there be you and me?
Why can't there always be us?
Together another day

I surrender to what may come

CARRIED

When what you hear is sadder than sad
And there is nothing you can do
You put your Cross in your heart
Relinquish what was

Carry on

You've known heaven
You've known hell

Carry on

Love is greater than love
Pain greater than pain

Carry on

When the rose becomes the flame
Fight has taken flight

Carry on

Never held back
All body
All soul
All in

Carry on

I hope
I focus
I accept
I reach out
Surviving and thriving

Carrying on

My love for you will configure the storm
Shape the sails
All warmth
My face is your clay

Carry me

Consecrate these shoulders in grace
My face is your clay
Slake this thirst
The rain makes rivers of us all

Carry me

Shape my cheekbones
My face is your clay
Shape my eyes to look with you
Every day of every life

Carry me

Love is greater than pain
It is made to be greater than itself
More than all suns burning eternally
More than sorrow beneath the tree
More than flight
More than speed
All plains and oceans into me
My eyes are made of your clay
Only look at me as you do

Carry me in you

My love for you is a kind of knowing
My love for you is a kind of dying
My face is all clay
Your face is rose
Your face is flame
Every day of every life
Heaven floats down upon us

Carry me
Carry me in you

IV. THE FOURTH DECADE: DEATH

"And the bells that I had heard in my room only moments before (my room where I have lived a whole life, where I was born and where I am preparing to die) seemed so clear to me; those same bells dragged their sounds like rags behind them over the swirling waters only to meet again without any recognition. It is still always that death which continues inside of me, which works in me, which transforms my heart, which deepens the red of my blood, which weighs down the life that had been ours so that it may become a bittersweet drop coursing through my veins and penetrating everything, and which ought to be mine forever. And while I am completely engulfed in my sadness, I am happy to sense that you exist, Beautiful. I am happy to have flung myself without fear into your beauty just as a bird flings itself into space. I am happy, Dear, to have walked with steady faith on the waters of our uncertainty all the way to that island which is your heart and where pain blossoms. Finally: happy."

—RAINIER MARIA RILKE, *LETTERS*

Reflections Ice Storm, by Carol Scott

COME WITH ME

Come with me before the world dies
It is pulling away
Shorelines broken down
Water-stretched droplets
Across an invisible web

Come with me before I die
I am waiting for you on some other side
I wish for rain
And it comes as your shape
Fallen around me

Come with me before the sun dies
Dense imploded rings of earth
Descend on your silhouette
Riddled with craters
Debris
Ruptured vaults of the long dead
Only the Now

Come with me before the universe cries
Heaves its last expansion
Of matter into ever darkening space
And it too becomes our atonement
Right before my eyes

Come with me before I die
I wait for sleep
And it comes as your shape
Overlaying my breasts as winding sheet

Come with me before the oceans dry
And there are no tears left to fill the seas
Your kingdom of God's fated play
Floating in the waters of me

Come with me before age shows its face

To move again
To move with hidden perfect chord
Inside one sound and one place

My soul
My soul
My soul is stricken
Sorrowful sickness
Too much love
My body can die
Let it die
But my soul is dying
What can be done?

Come with me before I die
Bring me to you
Brought into you
Undo the universe with a glance

IN DYING TIME

In dying time, the fruits fall from the tree
The leaves oblige and give way
You oblige the time to batter your face and hands

The sway of touch upon your face remaking mine
The wail of silent years falling unremarked in kind
Elegant in decomposition and rhyme

Things fall down, lower, lowly in space and time. Depths of oceanic memory

The seashells dropped from tiny hands fall below space and time, drown into Being, lower still Into the great silence of all breathing and of every year, inside the frail host that passes from your Kiss to mine

We are cast among them, wrapped in their perfume of cyclical retreat, languishing between Breeze and tide, forest and vale

Oblige me this time between the release and the ground, between the first breath and the great Repast, between the last leaves of autumn's dance and call, that twirl as they float
Lithe substances of grace descend as things do, down and down into me, into the clay and the earth of nature's consonant plea
Place your hands on my face, through my hair, all the way to the eternal salted sea of yellows And brightness remade

My dear sweet Lord of the forgotten and evermore, give your little lambs that which resides Between the blush of hesitation and the bruised head of resignation

Fall, fall to me, down into me, let me remake you my love, fall down into the first night before The retreat, below memory, beneath the first breathing

STARGAZER

You looked back at me
In the split second before heartbreak
Claimed what remains of my creation

At the very moment
My arms and legs
Readied themselves for starless night
You became more real
Than earth revolving around sun

Your eyes came to mine
At the last hour
Before the surface of the moon
Was worn smooth
When there would be nothing left
No inner wish to manifest
No lakes flowing into streams
Floating into the heavens
Sinking beneath my body
Into the purgatory nearing hell

In the last lonely passage
Of unremarkable time
Your perfect wisdom
Your happy smile
Replaced the hinge of my soul
That moves my body

You turned me inside out
At the very instant my chest
Had begun to sink
Residing closer to my spine
Compressing God's Word

Your breathing broods over the waters
Unmaking the land
Separate me into pieces

Wrapped and parceled out
Returned to your embrace

When you looked back at me
It pulled the sun closer
I am burning up in you
Shivering

When your eyes fell upon mine
The sun became everything
Except I cannot go on
Somewhere I must fold
Some hidden seam
Is written across my soul
I want to come home
To be inside your starlight
Burning away in you

I think back to the days of you
When the sun was large
Filled the windows
Warmed the curtain
Heated the glass
And everything tasted of lemon
And loving irreverence
But I cannot go on
Dissolving in my love

I need to remember
How you looked at me
The Seven Sorrows around your neck
Fallen on my breast
Igniting my tongue
To speak and to kiss
To kiss again
And my mouth could cover all of you
But I cannot go on

I am freezing to my bones in sky of black

My hands want your face
Your color
Your texture
Your uncharted face
The nebula of you
Ionized light inside light
Overwhelming matter and meaning
Let there be galaxies of you when I die
Universes of you

All matter, space, energy, and time
Are dying within me

How can I love you perfectly as you are?

SUNDAY'S CATACOMB

I plan to reacquaint myself with your bones
With the marrow of your bones
With the substance sponged on Christ's lips
In his Passion

At the center of the earth
I will find your bones
Bore into the marrow of the earth
With broken nails
Separated from my flesh
Tearing my fingers indifferently
My blood instinctually searching
Crying out
Gnashing the teeth of my bones
Wailing and smashed hands
Dug into graveled wall
Dripping towards your dried up bones

I will snatch you
Smuggle your bones out of caverned loss
Held under my dirtied shirt
Stuck to my chest in sweat and dried blood
Wet again, soaked in fevered longing
Shoulders beaten in stone
I will hold you
Nearest my beating weeping heart
Wild and savage
In my passion
Untrained squadrons of relentless rage
Untaught
Unable to learn
Clutching your bones to mine

Explorers we ought to be
Inside and out
Pick me apart
Do what you will

Scavenger whom I love
Untamed in longing

Make me your wreckage
Claim my bones for ash
Do what you will
Take haunted form
Rock me in the cradle
In feather down
Bones as brittle as birds

Today is Sunday
All the Churches bathed in blood
Blood of the Spring lamb
Bones torn inside out
Architectural bones
Breaking the centuries
Pulled together in Passion
Stone altar
Violent donative altar
Lay down your head
Loving altar of God's bone and flesh
Your flesh and bones and mine
For all time
Held to my chest
Passion

IN THE LAND OF MYTH

I cut your hair as you sleep
Weakening your resolve
Vanquishing you
Into me

Now I will be
Your insistent last thing
Fallen finely
As mist
At your feet

You will always be
The final minutes of my life
The verve of my moving touch
The striking sight

Relieve me of words and foolish deeds
Rearrange the verbs
On my vocal chords
Cueing me into silence
Fallen as mist at your feet

Verve of my beating heart
You may die tonight
Un-collect me
Collector of bones
Catacomb at the side chair
Drifting into ancient spell

Skin of the deity
Enshrouding you
Parched prayers
Singeing you
Dazzling in the lower quarter of night
Crawling into your labyrinth

Beautiful beautiful torn down body
With wings scattered to the outer wilds
Vanquish me
In your dying tonight

Un-collect me
Uncontested love
Your cheekbones run the gamut of my face
Ageless quartets in shatterless glass
I stare at the sun
Magnified and burned alive
In your undying light

Time has scratched its way into the cracks
Under the lids of my eyes
Sanded in sleep
Blind little body covered in sack

Quantify and ratify me
Reproach me
Holy hideous memory

Thawed desperate measure
Never the middle path
Every cup filled and dredging the sea floor
In the holy hideous mythic core

Beautiful beautiful torn down body
You may die tonight
Un-collect me
In triplicate prayer
Drain the cup dry

Little pomegranate tree
My flesh is taken to task
It will not last
How do you think I could be
The great repast
Gaunt as I am

Madness you are
Flooded with shunted star
How do you think
I can come to be
Fermented cherry in Eastern Sun

It is now five minutes past
Morning will not last
Sorrow dead on my lips
Twining your fingers in final lines
Prettiest tapestry
Weaving apart
Every thread of chance
Warding spirit of the soaked lance

Un-collect me lover preserved
Lover caught in the oil
Ambered passages
Without author
Landing in your marsh

Every year I shed my skin
Ornaments of me
For you

Beautiful beautiful torn down body
You will always be
The final minutes of my life
The verve of my moving touch
The striking night

UN-RANKED

How can I cling to life
In midday hour
In perfect heat
With fearsome need
Wafting over me

Strip me of my rank
Collected to the lowest rung
Animal faith
Unchecked in the last need
Washing over me

Division of bodies in deadly motion
Heavy artillery
Unloaded on the ground
Handful of dust
The lover's face
Hidden in your cosmos
Your breath
Your lung

Pooling, contusion of tears
Cooling my flushed face
Placating rank at your gate
Lovers unloved
Hidden in your cosmos
Of breath
Unsung

I have confused the end of hills
The start of lake
The bottom has fallen out
But makes no sound
I look out to leaves un-raked
Visages creaked and caked
Time winding its sensual decomposition
Of age and regret

Into me
Slowly and presently un-ranked

How can I cling to life
This tendered exchange
Outside your succession
As you drink the shining sea

Every one of your earths inhabited
Stringing me into outlawed reverie
Held firm in wooden beam
Your ferocity of need
Wanton little mystery
Stripping me of procession
Orderless and slouched beneath fallen tree

IF I COULD HAUNT YOU

If I could haunt you
Fill your body with me
If we could live forever in one body
I would bathe you in moonbeams
Your hair washed with mine
In citrus and myrrh
Honeysuckle still on the vine

Your body would be sweetness
Fresh and new
Your body would be an intoxicant of me
Within gardens of blue

My body will be your softness
My body will break the bough

Acres of green to run
Purpled forests at dusk
The pulling apart of husked corn
Delicate yellows
All seasons
Threaded into our shared body
But we are never undone
You'll be my color sinking to the floor

My body will pirate ships
My body will conquer Kings

Your fingertips will wrinkle only from days
Endless Mays and Junes of water light play
Pressed to my face
Your face
Running the ridges of your fingers
Down my spine

My body will lay down always on your bed
My body will never close and never die
Your soul haunting mine

THE WORD

I have come to the surface
Push me down again
Hands coated in proofed spirits
Firm on each shoulder
Pulsed into undertow

I cannot take meaning
The conceptions on hind quarter
Bearing down
Wailing wall of sound
Made impossibly
Preposterously into sense
Ancient deer cry
Stripped at its thigh
Into all thought

Expelled litmus test
Wanton word as orbiting star
Crucifying the deed
Hideously long reed
Plucked from middle lake
Turned into writer's pen
Every night debriefed again
Iniquity's den

I am still at the surface
Struggling for nothing
Sweet nonsense before man and God
But the passage is known too well
Unendurably swift and mortal
Vocal swell

Lands of eyelashes
Felled in triadic tear
Dropped to my moving lips
Spoken of love and grief and banalities
Vacant sound cut down
Word rising to the water's edge

Excruciating wisdom
The ship of fools has docked
Idiots and idioms
Unlocked designation of the dead
Bringer of mortality

Enunciated fatal blow
Truncated and bellowed
Animated animal caught in word
Crisp as bells
Sentenced to hell

Open your mouth
If you must. . . .

STILL . . .

We leave universes unfinished
Inside seasons of discontent
Imperfect love
Flawed in every way

Scattered cracked open seed
My heart shelled from yours
Food of birds

Still . . .

The balls of my feet curve at the sight of you
Toes outline your shape on fitted sheet
Cooler than icebox plum
Ambrosial to the pit
Bitten in heat

The song
The art
the dance
Remain in me
Replete with agony
Incomplete
Their maker forever dying of love
Stretched on the rack

Scattered cracked open seed
My art felled from yours
Food of birds

Still . . .

The soles of my feet run the gauntlet
Of my calves and knees
At the mere hint of your fragrance
Tossed ships at sea
Your musk upon my parting wave

Come to bed
Unreasoned love
Cascading red locks in dappled light
Ephemeral as whispered touch
Shaking the earth in laughter

Your melody caught on my teeth
My heart in your mouth
Your tongued melody
Catching me

The carving knife soaked in blood
The razor's edge with yesterday's shave
Glints of hair and foam
A patchwork of humming stone graves
Your handiwork appears and disappears

There is only so much you can take of me
Only so much you can take
Before I am gone

Still . . .

The arches of my feet
Peak the mountaintops
Plant your flags
All at the mere thought of you
Shivering in nudity

THE CATALOGUE

I awoke to find
My eyelids had disappeared
The immensity of things
Present everywhere
All objects recorded
Barreling down
Upon me

Every scintilla of matter and meaning
Invading the room
Thrust before my sight
Piles of paper reams
Bubbling under my vacant shoes
My feet bare
I collect the thicker soles
To withstand the heat
The sharp aridity
Barreling down
Upon me

The tacks from the box in the desk drawer
Spill out and come to every surface
These worn shoes have pulled me
Into the rug
Behind the sofa
Under the floorboards
Below the foundation
Into dirt
And still there is sun
Everything present
Barreling down
Upon my body
With heat
But still it is too cold

My hands barely keeping pace
The soil fills every crevice

Following patterns of hidden tributaries
As lace
And still I see everything
The sun remains below the earth
Where I am now
A passenger of your past compression
Upon my soul
Heated
But still it is too cold

My eyes burning
Unable to close
I press my hands upon them
But the light comes through every finger
I cannot cup my hands tight enough
The light seeps through the blinds
Everything present but you

Your books on the table
Two months of dust upon them
Your shirt still in the hamper
Folded paper in the pocket
Indecipherable scribbling
The piano bench unmoved
Your absence
Your inescapable absence
Your damnable absence
Demanding my presence

I put my hands over my eyes
The light still crawls through
Everything seen
All things but you

Death: The Shared Poetry of Artist Carol Scott and Caitlin Smith Gilson

Lace, by Carol Scott

DEATH IS NOT THE ENEMY

Death is not the enemy
Bad living is your foe
Blind in the headlights
Struck down body
Unpaid toll

Creation is not memory art
Life is beyond dying
Death is dueling partner
Friend not enemy

Bad loving
Misery must go

Boxed

The human eye cannot conceive
It cannot remember enough
To put together all the pieces

Essence now dust

THE YIELDING

Before I die
Let me swallow
The windows of my home
Magnificent drink of light

Let the crosses of the panes
Become my prayers of thanksgiving
For your grace
Within true rest and play

My place of rosary and rooms
Held in perfected time
Drifting into living heart
Living room of muse and art

Let my throat drink cold and crisp
Eternity present yet unseen
Spiritually sung elation

Let me watch the setting sun
Through windowpane

The universe comes to my door
Light of Cassiopeia
Water Bearers pouring forth
Welcoming most or only some
Where beauty is prime

Bemused
Laughter
Touched tears
Torched fears
Happiest poetic scribes
Singing the songs of life
Yielding in death to love

THERE IS DYING UNDERNEATH ALL MY LIVING

There is dying underneath all my living
Spending as fast as I am alive
Sucking the shadows
Peeling the fruit
Feeding me in segments
As I dream

What happens when I die?
Is heaven in the stars?
Will I look like me?

Moving dust
Star dust
My own dust

What happens to my friend
Who curves beside me
All visage but no face
In early light
I passed my reflection
On the face of the family clock

I can see my dying friend
I can see him shedding my skin
I look and he has gone
Wonderland once again

How long will it take me to turn to dust?
Will St. Peter meet me at the gate?
Will I know you?

Moving dust
Star dust
My own dust

Love triumphs over lust
Life resigning life

Dissolving my body
Into the bread dipped in Milky Way
Void divesting itself
In the last lighted day

Endless shooting stars
Falling at the end of time
Falling for each soul before and after mine

And you brighter than them all
Holding me as your draped pieta
Woven together heavenly body

POURED OUT

Death
Pouring out
Emptied
The glass is tipped
Broke on the floor
Liquid running contained no more
Once upright powerful
The tide has turned

You've pressed the glass to my face
But the last drop escaped
I cannot drink you enough
I stumble to the ground
Delirious
You stretch me out
I am watching the score
And it's getting late, so late
You clutch my neck and hesitate

There are things to be done
Everything must be finished
Body outing
Soul release
Devouring
Cleared to clarity
Dying to death
Fear of missing out
I am late I am late but I am never late

V. THE FIFTH DECADE: TIME

"And when night comes, and you look back over the day and see how fragmentary everything has been, and how much you planned that has gone undone, and all the reasons you have to be embarrassed and ashamed: just take everything exactly as it is, put it in God's hands and leave it with Him. Then you will be able to rest in him—really rest—and start the next day as a new life."

—St. Edith Stein, *Essays on Woman*

Crystal Ball, Tell Us All, by Carol Scott

TREVIGNANO ACROSS THE WAY

At final day
Knee deep in dance
Legs kicking the water
Out beyond the garden curve
To the very myth of you

You have come upon me
Floating unexpectedly
Fathomless dream
I dip my fingers first
Then my wrist
Into deep that calls upon deep

Where are you
Are you in the honey
In the garden chair
Hidden in the background
A portico of broken stair
A telescope to keyed-up stars

Are you
Ground down in my coffee
Mixed with steam and breeze
Shaved chestnut and cypress tree
My ferry to life after life

In every way
Roads left untraversed
Little bodies jumping from pleasing dock
Clearing the shallows
Trevignano gleaming across the way

Three towns
Drunk on unvarnished blue
I left my soul in the honey jar
Rowing out in search of you

Are you the stick of pine comb
The oar at my fingers
Green and purple figs
Wasps melting in the middle
Dying in the center of my flesh
Consuming as consumed
Encased in honey
Honey on my lips
Honey on my chin
Gliding sunset and straw
Feeding the animalesque

Two days have passed
I can still taste the wild fruit
Plucked from trees
Beneath the church

A day has passed
Blush peach assured of sunrise
Hours broken inside this cast
Once again
This day must fail
Puttering into sunset

For one moment I am
Sublime clean line
Displaced in your verdant hills
Of reasonless rhyme
Love lost beneath the shoal
A diamond pressed from coal

Cooled down heap of volcanic rock
Rolled into shoreline pebbles
And coarse grain sand
Each will exist
Long after I am gone

In some form
Beautiful one
Something else will remain

Every grey sand that sticks to my body
Freshly departing the water
I am
Redolent as the mist covering you
Far away in space without time

You have come upon my body
The storehouse of my soul
Unbolted portal
I cannot bear much more beauty
Willing heart leaps only so far
From the dock made of wood and stone

The shafts of every bone of mine
Ready to burst
To disintegrate into eternal joy
And perfect suffering

Every bone is breaking in its socket
Too much pressure in the air
Squeezed into my being
Beauty drowning me
Consuming me as I consume you

The wasp nest inside our flesh
Weeping and sighing for me
Make the Cross for me
Upon my face and chest
Untouched by time

No head furled back
In greatest delight is enough
To overcome this lack
Nothing but beauty can ready me
For your beauty

Rest me in your beauty
Age me in your beauty
Make me weak, jaundiced
An emptied basin to be filled
Let me burn up in heat
I will not compete
Dying in your beauty

At this final night
Sleep need not come
Invincible life
Perishing in your beauty
Consumed to be consumed

I am the honey-colored wasp
At the center of your flesh
Clearing the dock
Playing in heated wave

GOD BETWEEN THE LINES

Do you remember the hot house on the lake
With the bed raised on stilts
I could lean my feet over
Dangled as if peering down
From a dock into tideless water

These things have power now
They can take the heart right out of my chest
Inspect it
As if a package considered for transport
Turn it over, set it down, leave it for hours
All the while I lay out in memory
More dead than alive

Do you remember the garden
Behind the house in St. Ives
All the seagulls you fed
Just to make our children laugh
Masses of curled red hair in a thicket of play
Days of sun showers under canopy

Do you have any idea
What unseen weakness
Entered my blood stream
That day
Those days
Two decades ago
Laying dormant in my joints
In the places where muscle attaches to bone
Where movement begins and ends
And now it has such power of me
Everything
Everything conquered and divided
Drifting downstream

THE RECOLLECTION

The gentlest touches
Lifting the veil from youth into age
Skim my face as water's edge in shallow craft

In blinding sunshine I can recall the boat
Made of light golden browns
Polished wood now silken
The grain dissolved under hand long ago
Before I knew your name

How many times must you have sanded it down in cold off-season night?
There is room for one and together two
Folded in your way
Your pure knowing curve and fit
Of my own with you
When I knew you as you were

THE CHAR

Captivating little pomes
Without a pit
Popped whole
I can envisage the dross that remains
Macerated behind your heart
Where your organ lay
Drafted in your charcoal

The sumacs overgrown
Lording the rays in the courtyard
Behind the low door
Berries sticking of indigo
Glazing your mother tongue
Drafted in your charcoal

You've rounded my heart down
Curiously
With the letter opener which lays about
On the wooden writer's desk
A Leviathan of middle room
Drafted in your charcoal

Camouflaged hide
Bone trim handle of antler
Deer or elk
One unrepeatable animal majestic
Broken for game
Violent, elemental, elegant
Without name
Skinned in earliest hour
Drafted in your charcoal

All image today and forever
All image over word
Image over dying
Image placating miles
Image inside the sweeter cry
Parting image
Image of your hands
Image of foreign lands
Always you

Image of your legs walking to the shower
Image under thigh collecting all of mine
Image of your finest hour
Image of contoured knee
Image undying
Always you

Image for the bed of recollect
Image as risen dough
Image of buttered bread
Image of your ceiling as I sigh and sigh
One Image as I die

Drafted in your charcoal

IN MY BEGINNING

To lay my head on your shoulder
In a dreamland of rain
To raid the warmth of your bed
Under the window square and wide
Unpainted trim, greens and blues
Curtains neglected brushed aside
Everything but you

The covers once again as tents to raise and hide
Chase me with laughter
Blushing all over as roadside bridal roses
Collect at my feet
Blushing down into my soles
Pine needles under foot
Chastened in play
Under you

But your watercolors trail down
Claim no substance
Caress everything and nothing
The rain cannot compete
A haunting mist of colors
Dimmed into sleep

WHAT PRECEDES

Before thought resides touch
And it is all hers to give
She with the small hands

Only two seashells find place in her palm
Fingers cupped as cheekbones jut
Each finger bone the conductor's bow

What little hands to brush past emptied lands!
Stretched towards her needlepoint
The breads pulled apart, heated joy
The tender embrace at doorstep home
The honeycomb upon the hurt

And it is all hers to give and take
But she never takes
She with little hands of life
Wands remaking every duality into light

For mortal eyes it is a spell
A transposition of desert into azure blossoms
Falling as snow
as lace
as sound
as engines dying down
and revving up
and blues that hurt, that court the dead with tender shades to resurrect
even the lost-hearted foe

Her beauty spreads its love letters like legs in sand
The cobalt comes close,
touches,
and then farther may it go

Caressed by parted lips and the littlest of hands

CALYX

Little downed dream with kisses on the tongue
Intoxicating the boundary with your languishing howl
You are the end of man and woman
An apocalyptic vision
Throwing me to the wolves
Taking me to the flame
Tossing me with the wood
Into the margin thin relief raised in every grain

Forced shivers of silvered mercury
Tracing my back along the wall
Raiding me of my sighs with silken tones
Pounded and carved sunken relief
Low and high
Imperious height and depth
Every sculpted efficacy entrancing as fingers pry
Raping the edge of the thorn
Leaving only the sap
To drop down cupped calves and thighs

A sorcerer of cherried sex
Despoiling my legs treading the air
Playing nonsense and pretense
Playing with death as plaything hurled high

The end of sky and ground
The end of man and woman

The air as chaser drunk down to the dregs
Stings the tongue and burns the throat
Your lips taste of all smoke and oak
My waist wasted down

These gapes in anatomy ply irresistibly into deep curve
Once upon a time my ribs were pulled apart until I was yours
You have my heart
A toy for your feet, for your teeth, for your conjuration

Crushed and remade without image
In darkest morning

THE WAGER

Each year
A delinquent ecstasy
Wraps a tangled tome upon my throat

Each year
Obscene against my arms
Rounds my chest
Braced waist and down
To the browned and desolate earth

Another year falls to my knees
I pant and cry
Walled off yellowed cries

Heavy years pick apart the seam from the dressing gown
One by one
Stitch upon stitch
Plucked and debrided of its place
Flattened and chided
Unsewn by you

Undo the first of me and the last of me
The first and the last
Render me reckless in your wake
Undo the first and last things
From last to first
Curl me up
Pack me away
Folded into the basement box

Year upon rolling year rolling towards your oblivion
Dark green hill blended eventide
The primordiality of lies
Resides between truth and rented air
Tear out the year from the page
Word forgotten
Word unsaid or said in the stumbled dead end
Unsaid

Every year brushes its fingers through my hair
Take the in-between and turn me inside out
Everything unsettled at the seams
Worn down wishful haunted little dreams
Littler into the winter of each year
Into the snowflake lake of ice and still
The hunter's chill upon my cheek
Till dust has us at its mercy for the tiny and the meek

At the center of each year
The infant pant and cry
Land my life in the glint of your eye
Enclose it in one gloss and shine
I am not worthy of life nor death

But please, please one year all the same
One more bat squeak of time
By which the things that are forever yours are mine

IN THE TIME OF UNFORGIVING

Let me tell you a story
Tucked and buried beneath the evening tree
Dappled with candled lights and wanderlust brushes against the cheek
All art and decay cast below the rhythmic wheel
The dealer's face drawn with darkened blue
And you, you have come in from the long haunted wood

But the story escapes me my love
It consecrates time as it flees the open window
The cracked door
The spaces between
The words come and go, traipsing upon my toes
Entering my feet and in the leave tide of my lips

The story escapes me
Lovers on lamplit streets
Loosely rearrange the lore on my lips
Unfold the winding cloth and wrap it around my hips
Sink your teeth and taste the fresh-cut fields
Rummage through my veins
Pull my half-cocked embrace into pulse
Pull me to the water's edge
Make a boat of my body
Oars of my bones
Close my eyes with one stroke of your hand
Every lash separate and intact

But the story is not here
It is across the crater lake
At the center of the wishing well
Above and below where you are now
The secretive chapter, the passage unlined
In my time of undying, say sweet words
The sweeter nonsense
The sweetest nothings
Words that hover and dance and never resist the brink

Tell me a story
Never signal depth nor time
Neither space nor memory
Lightly, lighter
Softer than daylight dream, across the lake
As wide as sea
Held above memory
Outside the brutal yoke

A story
A brighter vessel
One story without word
Falling unremarked in the dew

Time: The Shared Poetry of Artist Carol Scott and Caitlin Smith Gilson

Flutes, **by Carol Scott**

WHAT I KNOW FOR SURE

What I know for sure
The constant in life is change
Surprise me
Beguile me
Wild me
I am in Plato's cave
Chained to a zero
Offend me
Bend me
Love me
Tomorrow is now
Today is yesterday
Is this a Fellini movie?

What I know for sure
I cannot change without you
Counter me
Disrobe me
Unmask me
Be the descent of the dove
Tethered to its wing
Shackle me
Bind me
Blind me
What is now fails tomorrow
La Dolce Vita?

WHAT IS YOUR STORY?

Everybody
Has a story
From beginning
To end

The moments/mundane
Minutes marked/forgotten
Time of pleasure/pain
The making of a life

Experience through senses
Favorite tastes and smells
Sounds
Sights
Touches

Touched at the beginning
Touch at the end

Did your dreams come true?
Were you the dreamless?
Who dreamt of you?

Ego as delicate as egg
We're you scrambled/hard boiled
Raw hanging from a nail
Part of a beautiful hollandaise rich/buttery

Living can be cruel
Untouched at the beginning
Untouched at the end

What happened to you?

Were you loved in the dark and in the light?
Touched from beginning to end?
Kissed with sweet presses?

Untouched loving dream
Did your dreams come true?

Did you overflow into sex and laughter?
Were you defeated by sin?
No happily ever after?

Written in the palm of your hand
Was yours like mine?

Did you live in a mansion/in a box on the street?
A box soon in the ground?

Were you dreamless?
As I dreamt of you

Practiced in virtue
Blessed by family/friends
Defeated by sin
Lonely asking for death

End
When your life is done
Will it have been well done?

LIFE, DEATH, AND LIFE AGAIN

Opened eyes
Compelled to look
Beauty commands
Fairytale as truth

Time drags its metal hook
Across the sand, floor, door
Thrashed apart
As cut-down trees

Every second passed, a life elapsed
Strange stranger of the past
How long will I last?

Perfected in glory
Carrying heaven in my heart
Art demands
Physical body
Love pronounced

Secret time
Loving peace
Hand on my head
On my breast
Release
Time so interior
It becomes the heat
Of your beating heart
From kiss to kiss
Beauty
Reprise

MY SKIN REMEMBERS YOU

My skin remembers you
More than my mind
More than my heart

Everything in the end is flesh
Bodies reworked
Thawing ice

All memories
Are the sensation of you
Before I knew
Before I understood
Before I recognized fear and age
Before I touched parting
Before I felt what breaking away does
Before you forgot my name

Both my body and soul
Left to themselves
Half apart and still close
Collecting memory

Fading half-thoughts
Till the mind goes dark
Lingering perceptions unclear
Your touch as my skin
More than my soul
More than my spirit

My skin keeps reminding me of you
Raising itself into shivers
At your sight
Even when my eyes shut down
Descending into every night from now
Until my body gives out
Gives up its ghost

THE SIXTH DECADE: ART

"Every work of art causes the receiver to enter into a certain kind of relationship both with him who produced, or is producing, the art, and with all those who, simultaneously, previously, or subsequently, receive the same artistic impression. . . . To take the simplest example; one man laughs, and another who hears becomes merry; or a man weeps, and another who hears feels sorrow. A man is excited or irritated, and another man seeing him comes to a similar state of mind. By his movements or by the sounds of his voice, a man expresses courage and determination or sadness and calmness, and this state of mind passes on to others. A man suffers, expressing his sufferings by groans and spasms, and this suffering transmits itself to other people; a man expresses his feeling of admiration, devotion, fear, respect, or love to certain objects, persons, or phenomena, and others are infected by the same feelings of admiration, devotion, fear, respect, or love to the same objects, persons, and phenomena. Art is a human activity consisting in this, that one man consciously, by means of certain external signs, hands on to others, feelings he has lived through, and that other people are infected by these feelings, and also experience them."

—Leo Tolstoy, *What Is Art?*

Magnum Opus, by Carol Scott

THE DIVINE ARTIST

I am shipwrecked in your claret
There is no finality to the glass
I trespass and peer into your infinity
Corundum red and sanguine fed
A deadheaded bud
Cellared in your amatory of arms

*What have I done
Asking you to make me helpless?*

You are endless ether
The erotic exordium
The entrancing of flesh without end

Your colors breed thoroughbreds
And burst as grapes in willing mouth
Unlaced shapes intoxicate mere sight
Sinless blues under cover
You touch my chin
Wipe away the wine
Wildflowers
Nectar
I cannot contain

I am without power
Make your paint from my exquisite pain
I spill forth in pigment
A train of color and light
The inquisition of hues
Descend my ribs and back
Pricked and set alight
I am yours happily bewildered
Bereft of sense
Under your glass and without defense

Exorcise my blood as your paint
Mix my body and soul

Till time knows no end
In the simplest crystal bowl

The master releases the servant
Dropped at her feet
Reclining in rhapsody
I am your foundling excavated
From stretched molasses
And ancient peat

What have I done
Asking you to make me helpless?

You are the sacred litany of crystalline glass
Lean bone China white
Your grace is a hammer
Your virtuosity has walloped my knee
Incapacitated in sensuous sighing plea
Chaliced art of blown kisses
You have pounded the life out of me

You are hovering as I sleep
The shadowed cloud
Impenetrable
Making me turn the hand of fate
Robbing me of the lesser things
And easy facts
You've wrought roses from dust and clay
Made stems as cathedral naves

I had no idea what I asked for
But I shall ask for more
You command me
I am down on shattered knee
Take the hammer to my stomach
And the other knee
Beat the life out of me
Into me
Through me
The Cruciform three

What have I done
Asking you to make me helpless?

Your beauty overflows into me
I thought I knew how to die
I have no dying that could compete with you
No dying within me that can complete
The stakes you have long wagered

Take me to glass
Burn the life out of me
Make me flowers dipped in sap
Greedy for water
Terrify me into tenderness trailing down
Your canvas of ecstasy

Your causation confounds me
I had no dying that could compete with you
I am yours under glass
Reflected again and again

What have I done
Asking you to make me helpless?

In your wild dismemberment of mediocrity
I am but a novice at your door

THE LANTERN

Yesterday my lantern broke
And my spirit leapt outside my soul
My soul beyond my body
Heavenly one
You are at the most mortal part
Of my heart

Everything
Everything that I am
Leapt outside of time
And returned through you
Broken lantern
Poured back into me

When I saw your creation I wept

I am skipping stones with my very life
Ecstasy crept back inside my house
My mind
My cuffed and drummed body
Bruised my baking breaking soul
Returning through you
Light of my lantern

Wood of the Elm
Wood of the Pine
Wood of the Coffin
Wood of the Cross
Everything on fire
I am skipping stones with my very life

When I saw your creation I wept

You advance the Divine Word
With hum and verve
Exuding charity and light
Love and light

Lantern of light
Surge of light
Surfing light
I'm skipping stones with my life
Everything
Everything that I am
Returning through you

Carry me to your bay of paint
Dipped in your font
I drop the gown of my birth
Into your creation
Holy evocation of your imaged elation

When I saw your creation I wept

You've struck a blow
To the most mortal part
Of my heart
Everything
Everything I am
Wept with fire
When I saw you create

Your art is sacred fragrant sensation
Rained downed raspberries
Wet on the eyes of my tongue

When I saw your creation I wept

Crested gardenia
Blooms at night
Pulled down stars
Topless trees
Smooth silken sheen
Of your fingering
Light
Dappled thing
Never dry of tear
Your art is awe without fear

When I saw your creation I wept
I made tear-fall
Tears and tears
Always replenished by release

Some great God
Must have sucked your honey pot
Tongued your toes
Kiss your fingertips
To create like this
All blaze and bliss

Some great God must have broke and broke
Your lantern in the throes
You're too good not to be consumed
Not to be returned to the fire
Not to live again

When I touched your creation I wept
I wept myrrh
I wept
Everything under fire

IL REGALO

How many gifts are we given
Before the very first collection of matter
Crowds around the invisible inlet
Making us individual and living?

Our bodies would disintegrate
Should we try to know such love
Caressing every bend
Of our seconds in this life

The gifts I do know
The ones you have given me
Beloved friend
Saved me from the desolate constant
Day and night

I am hushed breath of disbelief
I have loved your gift before I was born
And will love you
When I am scattered as dust
Your gift is this trust

Your love has upheaved me from depth
Animated my heart with hidden tune
Sung before the earth ever groaned in pain
Before it recoiled at its nearing end

My happy soul has gone under
The whitest part of the wave
It's lost itself in joy
Drowned itself in your gift

My soul within yours
Can feel without its body
It can touch the Corpus
Make the sign of the Cross

My soul alongside yours
Sips transcendent love
It weeps without eyes
Embracing you as pure gift

My soul has feet
Subterranean as pine tree root
My soul collects you in the inner ring
That last saw sun over two thousand years ago
When Christ hung on much longer
Deeper than he should
Farther than any blessing could ever descend

We are not worthy of such gift
But it is passed on through you
Dearest friend
Tributary of Beauty and Passion
Gift of my finally formed heart
Raised into loving unction

My companion of unmeasured mystery
My soul has kissed your eternal truth
Surviving death through your embrace
Impossible happiness as gift
Flowing with baptismal promise

Agencies of lonely towers
Broken down by you
You have give me a soul
That can feel without its body
The once lonelier longing
Hollowed by hand and hour
Washed clean and bright

This pure gift of our tears
Breaks open the moment
It meets soft warm skin
Held to mine in sweetest weeping

In your gift
I now know the very substance

Which lined my first tear
Shared with the One
Who is Love itself

THE ARTIST

The artist has come home with hands
Dipped in myth and citrus-sweet death
Land me in your well
Obsidian sheen
Chasmic spaces leaned and trimmed
Planetary bodies spread between sheets of fiber
Sheets of cotton
Lit into brilliance in your muscled flaxen blue

Fiendish rapt play with light and shade
Thriving on the bewitchment of scene
Spires fetishized into form

The artist bewitches the in-between
The crystalized dislocation of joints
Bodies rolled around in shine and silk

The artist has come home
With hands dipped in holiness and hushed sighs
The long-supplanted fairytale
A trail of breadcrumbs for little birds

What would I give to be your artifact caught in sap?

The artist has come home
Standalone world galloping into ecstasy
Taming the animal into spirit, the spirit into river
All things shivered by your glassy vision
The sap hardened into lake
The artist's recourse knows no firmament
But the laying down of arms

All things lay below the artist's hands
Tension waiting for creation
Sinew and ligament curled and smoothed
Shouldered into the freeze
Then everything breaks
The floodgates
Amber warmth of hues in morning steam

Every angle and beam
The incandescent life

The artist's hands dipped in the little death
The artist's hands in eternalizing sex
The artist's hands in the surrender which only gods command

What would I give to be your artifact caught in sap?

THE BLUE

Waste me and disturb my every bone in your deepest, redolent blue
Tiny petals separated one by one in distinction
Into the blessing of your hue
Filled to form in your fingertips
Delicate as lace and then wrought into shape
Rigid, relaxed, and curved back
Against sun and shade
Untouched
Retouched
Casted youth
Brace my hips rocked back and forth
As pendulum clock ticks the final stay
Your shaded downy sapphire clue
Hidden in every stroke
Too perfect for skies and seas

Waste me and disturb my every bone in your deepest, redolent blue
Drip me away into sucked embers
Blown I am
I am panted death into life
Heated sighs
Ravaged and cooler

The stilled saddened loss stands within the shaded blue
Behind softened hills that fall into the bay
My youth foraged away
Curled and peeled back to the bend
Your fingers dripping with honey and other such fragrant ends

Draw the maritime far away land of body and soul into the canvas of your heart and mine
Time has never been nor will be anything other than blown kisses through teeth
Breached, expelled, brought into light in your perfect, sweetest, heart-breaking blue

Today, the wild jasmine perfumed the hills
Today its memory long spent the burning night into day
And I was eternity and time

THE VISIONARY IN HIGH CONTRAST

Have I shattered you indestructibly?

What could that mean
To be broken and unbroken
In the maker's dream

The contraries roll down your sharp inseam
The part of your thigh where legs parry
Uncoupled and un-complied
Where words trounce the article
Heaving the past participle
Juiced
Jumped
Sexed and roused
Everlasting splinters of you
That is what means to batter your love eternally

Have I blown out your windows and your knees?

Fattened glorious honeybees
A harem hive of pieces shining, stacked
Every article pushed aside
The present is under attack
The past is not a participant
It is your lack
The spectacle is always reflecting back

Have I bartered your reflection in the glass?

Your fool's paradise cast against time
Numberless spheres of ice pelt the window
Surprising in Spring
To have such a torrent
Bring you through to me
Violent squall busting the mirror
Still the bees buzz home
Translucent passage into the nectary

Let me shatter you indestructibly
Into future
With no past participle
Or article
Or parried thigh
But skies
Arresting and contesting
Jumping
In the vastness of glass there is always guise

TO PAINT IN HEAVEN WITH YOU

To paint in heaven with you
What else could I do?
But look forward to age and loneliness
To love the loneliest of silent night
Monastic corridors of time winding down
As staircase to dying light
To welcome weakness of earthly sight
Another sort of holiness
In your storehouse of daydream

Your hands as visions upon mine
Inhabiting my fingers
Possessing them in midnight visitations
Curving them to your Will
Ten nimble bodies resurrected
You place me with face
You replace my hands upon my face
The ghost of you
My fingers in tawny paint
In the blue of kisses
Hewn wishing wells
Coins dropped in longing for the quiet death
Even pain
Pain will do
If it brings me nearer to you

To paint in heaven with you
What else overwhelms angelic sight?
Washed clean in your bright blessed beauty
Your peace and prescient colors
Where greens happily weep yellow
Weep coriander
Weep citrus peels
Everything in threes
The scent of bread in olives and oil
And riots of reds
Your colors as horses

Drinking from streams anew
Where the wildflowers weave and play
Each a daybed to lay my head recovered
In your colors of light, stables, farm-stand fruit and sun
My head upon your shoulder
In the inviolate red

To paint in heaven with you
Is to enjoy even the grave
And the gift of petal upon the stone
Softer now
Slower too, but come
Come home
Pressed lips on cooled skin

If only heaven had your paint
My bones would be yours
As brushes dipped from beginning to end
In your font of redeeming blue

NARCISSUS IN GLASS

What furnace of heat
Must come upon the body
To melt and make pliable
The prologue of crystal
The epitaph of glass

Transparentized hills of Venetian glass
Thinnest sheaths of heat
Stretched to outlast
Teams pulled apart into clarity
Narcissus peering into lake

Closing shrine of spirits encircle
Your reflection surfacing for air
Breaching the water in refracted light

Who drowns in reflected love
Who dies in the flowing Spring
Reflected back
Who cannot distinguish your eyes
As they are mine
Refracting the light

We run fingers across the beveled ridge
The traveler is seconds away
The clock does not tick
No execution
It has been given stay
It wades in the water as baptismal font
Sinless shine
Thick and narrowed
Height and marveled depth
Ovidian past

What furnace of heat must
Come upon the soul
To be so hot

Then inanimate and cold

Dizzying hills under hand
The lights that never quite land
The peaks dip into valley
Here there is no shadow of death
But coral and reef
Innocence regained
The Impossible reframed
The sun roped and pulled to earth
In the demitasse of glass

Who drowns in reflected love
Who dies in the flowing spring
What furnace of heat must
Come upon the body and soul
To shine impossibly new
Amorous gods in lighted fold

MY CHILDREN: THE ONLY LASTING ART

My children
Every essence of all the good
Packed in fragrance
I could be shot through with mortal arrow
It could pierce my heart
Rip my bones apart
And I would be everything
Everything that happiness is and should be
Loving them

Art: The Shared Poetry of Artist Carol Scott and Caitlin Smith Gilson

Full Throttle, by Carol Scott

HER TUMBLER OF GLASS

Cubism's naughty little dream
Ice then steam
Hands dipped clean
Butterflied dress
Glass caressed
Made for fingers cupped
Dangling unresponsively
Over the loveseat
Nearing sleep

Lux fiat in the crossfire night
Liquored delirious light
Reflected intensity
Backdrop of mahogany
Thousands of rivulets
Each cut in fearful time

She commands the blinding wheel
The descending couplet
Acres of colorant
Miles of thrice-carved crystal
Compressed in shocking sight

Arcobaleno
The cupola's gravitational pull
Color on color
The light pirouettes by heated flame
Let them eat cake
Round her blameless fingers
Wrists and ankles

She swims above the reef
Watching her reflection
Facets of piquant light
Tastes of latticed pie
Raspberries and cream
Wine mellow, without sting

Eat up
Life is a feast
The pearl is in the oyster

ART AS FOOD

The artist
Separates ache
As quietly as flour is sifted in pan
Only the finest grains remain
Readied for her hand
Dipped into Angelic tongue
Oil of incarnation

Body of art
Food of gods
Rising debriding pain
Sorrowful leagues of underwater sigh
Pleasure enjoined
Bright as precious coin
Separated without notice in the night
As gold from dust

Her work begins
Morning before light
Gardenia in fatal bloom
Every dying delight
Resurrected
Wafting into her sun-soaked room
Spellbound broken bread

Panis Angelicus
Art as food
She fills the bellies
Satiates the soul
See and taste

Crust of bread
Soaked in milk
The sweetest synesthesia
Tasting her paint
Crumbs of cake
Scooped in hand

The confectionery of cherubs
Your kingdom come
Under cathedral dome

THE ARTISAN

Every civilization has art
Ramped up egos
Twilight of idiots and idols
Sainted mosaic faces
Holy light retracing the dead

Man creates art
Willful splendor
Paths of gold
Complexions of love and loss
Civilizations at war

Dislocated forms
Whiplashed norms
Forms enjoined
Gilded riots of color adorned

God creates man
Savage beauty
Salvaged mysteries
Immortality on stretched canvas

Oh! How glorious to be an artist!
Spending days aesthetically engaged
Discovering muses at your door
Inspiration
Beauty personified
Power restored

Creation not as God but from God
Let there be light
Finding yourself by being yourself
Other than self
Original
Not a copier
A doer who also dreams
A maker of things

Melodic song of poetry and rhyme
Colorful bends of paint
Marble and form
An aesthetic quest
The blessed best

Oh! How glorious to be an artist!
To be the Beautiful
Meaning beyond seen
Sight beyond sight
Heaven on earth

WRITING PARTNERS

I ask for it all
I could not wait for you
For you to read my words
It is breathing my thoughts

Our words volley, play
I ask for it all
And it comes
Against loss, loneliness, sadness

I was in the wilderness
I wanted nothing more than to be
Than to play
Three days in the desert
I could not wait to be with your words
Our words magnetizing the other

I ask for it all
Breathing words into the air
Hurricane winds blowing
Dizzying my brain with intoxication

The spirit oozing through every pore
Love
Making passion to celebrate
The act of creation

THE SEVENTH DECADE: PRAYER

"Art and prayer are the only decent ejaculations of the soul."

—Joris Karl Huysmans, *The Damned*

Dome, by Carol Scott

THE PSALMIST'S EARLY LAMENT

Your innocence disrobes me
It confuses the time and the flowers
Each drifting in and out of the other
Hours recast upon your face
Opening and closing the day
The streams that mingle into rivers
The eventide song seems to cascade as doves into bells
Forever into you
Littlest of lovers unbeknownst to themselves
Uncut, ever uncut, by the trail of vanity and grief
Carving its curvature into every other feature and face
But yours

Your innocence undresses me
It places my body into wildflowers
Reconfigures my spine and my breath
Never again another early death
The gentle blessed steam off crisp morn and earthen air
The land felled and the scent of hay and coal
The earth which moves to your walk and smile
The unending perfumed land
The light without shadow
The hill after hill and vale of brightness in your face
The lost foal found at your arm
Placed at your side
Come hither, come near
Place me into the stream, river, and steam

The earth need not obey for it knows only you
The sky need not obey for it sighs only for you
There is neither dust nor ash, there is only you

In the time preceding all weeping, the earth and sky come home to you
My lips unclothed of all word and deed retreat into themselves relentlessly for you

In the time of first weeping
I stand to kneel at your feet

In the time of endless cries
I search the deep upon deep of the psalmist's cavernous plea
I follow the crickets homing sound
Reverberates my chest and bends the knee
Into the hollow
Into the small
So far have I searched for you and find myself undone
My lonely love who alone in the quiet moves love

LINES TO GOD BEFORE SLEEP

What earthquaking presence of beauty
In this passing moment
When I knew you as God must love you
As if the trees are lit with thousand fireflies
And masses of cinnamon clouds
Raid heaven with heaps of fragrance
Leaping out of the womb

At this moment
With more passion
Than rolling bodies
I desire to be holy and good
To be age renamed
Pure as wild lilies fed on sun
And all my blood replaced with water
All my body light
My sight covered with your two hands
And I could kiss you
Before my foundations crumble
And then mingle my dust with yours

You are the Good and the Beautiful
You walk and even the stones weep
Under your feet
In gratitude for their semblance of being
But I live and breathe and love
I am not worthy of you

I am not worthy for you
To enter under my roof
For you step on my chest
To push me into your grace
To carry me to the grave
But only say the Word
Touch me with your Word
Pummel and ravage me
With your Word made flesh

And I shall be healed
To love you as you are

BRUTISH PRAYER

Ruthless prayer
Words transcribe beads
Recording care
Transfixed into swan
Beneath water yet breathing air

Ruthless
Razor sharp unmerciful prayer
Dashed hopes
Sinking below
The one-way path of long ago

Crossing deserts of nothing
Repeated nothing
Mounds of the inconsequential nil
For you
Body of nightly prayer
Laying your weight on me
Mercilessly cruel cross of prayer

Liveries standing at the vacancy
Litanies of annihilating features
Prayer without word
Word without prayer
Loss enumerated
Unenumerated cost
Down into the chamber of execution
There is nothing but prayer

Your substance of myrrh
Feathered into the air around my pillow
As I sleep but do not dream

You metamorphosize perfection
Petulant prayer
Incessant
Ever-present prayer

Shying the moon
Tossing the galleons at sea

Almost heinous
Obscene to be this impregnable
To be filled with your love
Profane prayer
Run your rough wooden finger
Down my cleft into the hidden there

Through the bead
Decades upon decades of prayer
In need
Slowed into ugly brutish prayer

You are the repeated nothing
Feathered into the air around my pillow
As I sleep but do not dream

You implode mountains with one event
Remaking consent
Corseted tones of prayer
Effortless interior descent
Condemn me into earthquake
Demanding inviolate ancient prayer

There is no choice but your sun
Your fire
Your spectral depth of lake
My skin bubbling over into black stone
Forsake me
God of gods
I cannot take your prayer
This heavy heart still beating as it is staked
Falling in line
Into mouthed word and prayer

You implode the mountain into cavern
Lowering my remains
Into the center of the earth
Where none can reach me but you

Consummate thief of my heart
The four chambers keep repeating
Echoing the other
Ceaseless lonely conversation

How can prayer save?
Preposterous prayer
It neither soothes nor stills
Imposter prayer
Thief of the art of memory

I remember candied sliced almonds
Sweeter things
Play in sand and rain
Feathered into the air around my pillow
As I sleep but do not dream

There is no rhyme
Or reason
Or right season to pray
And this is precisely the point
I sleep but do not lay
I stand while I sit
What is up is down
The wise are as contorted as clowns
I am drowned to be saved

Sage of agony
Your mercy is forged in fire
Its smoke choking me
Feathered into the air around my pillow
As I sleep but do not dream

A LITTLE PRAYER

Of all the powers in the world
There is nothing more pure
Lovelier still
Than incarnate shyness before the Great
The True
And the forever Good

As tears fill the seven seas
You replenish God's most precious Beauty

You are the food of elegy and understanding

THE GAME

If there is one thing I can do
It is play tricks on you

Gamboling in subtext
Creatures of subtler sex
Bonfire vanities
Games that test one's sanity
Tame your tragedy into resignation
You are the age of hesitation

Clues in astral cards
Red and blue
Diamond hues
I am the joker un-removed
The prettiest rage of blushed cheeks
On silent stage

If there is one fate I see through
It is to load the deck with you

In every game there is a court jester
A tester
The spiritual molester
The carrion bird and unknown contestant
Who strips it raw
The meat from its side

If there is one phrase I can say
The end of all day is already in play

Every pastime is done
Under God and sun
So be warned
The game is in play

Les jeux sont faits. . . .

To both foe and friend
Futurity's game has already been played
Splayed out
As bride and corpse
Mother and child
Whore
Penitent to her pore

You must play chess alone
It is your turn
Not mine
I'll checkmate you in sultry sigh
Your joker un-removed

Daedalus jetting
Un-forgetting
Hands as mountains
Commandeering Icarus
In his conceit
If only there were a game
To relieve his fallen fame

Les jeux sont faits. . . .

THE DOUBLED PRAYER

Your cardamom aura
Doubles down
In the last leg of the race
The smell of lemon and peppermint
And camphor balm rubbed on bared shoulders

The vulnerable bones project
Hint of latch and door
To the secret room
Beneath the winding stair
Padlocked
Without a key
Double down
Nothing is fair
Everything is laced
Drunk on the viper's stare

Skin scarlet with Helios
Charioting from East to West
The god of the unsung simmering blood
Driven hip slung
Casting bands of tangerine
Between the seas of blue
Ransacked summer
Defeating the sexton
Burning up the dew

You are the wager against every holed-up want
Pulling the paper off the wall
Stripping the paint
Sledgehammering the decorative divider
Separating rooms
There goes the load-bearing wall

There is no in-between
You've leaned out the grasses

Clean and strong
Naked in your touch

There is no in-between
There are only a series of nows
The now has come and gone
Fallen off the cliff
I never knew how
To foul you out
To beat you at your game
God, double me down

YOUR PRAYER IS COARSE WOOD

Your prayer is coarse wood
Rough as parched mouth
Days without water
Delirious for death

Divine silence
Why do you abandon me as I kneel
Finally for you

The floor is smooth and cold
It reminds of lake and diving well
Of abundant water spilling from lips
But I am days without water
Hanging on your perfumed rose hips

Your promised earth as it is in heaven
Has invaded the disks of my spine
You are contorting me in and out of time
Drinking sand from stone
I've lost my mind in your prayer
In your promised love

Tempestuous awful causation
Your sorrowful decade
Rips wide my spleen
Snatches the silver
Feasts on my insides
Gutted as fresh catch
A fisher of men

Divine silence
Why do you abandon me as I kneel
Completely for you

How do you expect me to pray
When I cannot breathe
When I am bleeding out

When the water is mud and dung
My lungs are gills
And you have pushed me to the ground
Your catch
A fisher of men

How can I lay down
How can I stand
How can I hear your voice
Are you answering me
Commanding me
My insides are out
These lungs are slits at my neck
Opening and closing
The mud cannot be sifted from the water
Where are you fisher of men

There is no water
I am days without it
Days without water
I thirst terribly
Searching for you
Panting deer in deepest forest
Waterless fish

Divine silence
Why do you abandon me as I kneel
Entirely for you

Come here
Crawl into my bed
Show me your prayer
Finger the beads for me

Do you have any clue
How to put me back together again
Divine seducer
Awful wildness of prayer

Your graces
Have cleansed my youth

Washed it out
Your thumb squeaking the glass
Pressing with breaking force
I will not last

Divine silence
Why do you abandon me as I kneel
Desperately for you

Down me with my last drop
Of water to wine
Wine to blood
From Cana to the Cross
Loaves and fishes
Give me something to eat and drink
I am days with emptiness

How do you expect to put me back
When all the king's men failed
How can you put me back together again
My lips are dissolving into dust
Days without water

Divine silence
How can I pray

ONLY SILENCE CAN I GIVE

Only silence can I give
My silence is love
It abides in you
As atmosphere

One drifting snowflake
Glanced in windowed sight
My offering of love
As silenced night

One wall may be added
In my cherished room
I leave it bare
Until you fill it
Un-beating chamber
Held still
In wait for you

Sleep of the great silence
Underwriter of thought and memory
Moving through the keys

Sleepless angels watch over me
Christ's keeper of torment's mystery
House of my soul

Downward forest of the great forgetting
I do not know you
But you know me
Have I come far enough?
Will I lay down my life?

When will you come for me
Dream of the great silence
Sleep of the boundless dream?

Prayer: The Shared Poetry of Artist Carol Scott and Caitlin Smith Gilson

48 Shades of Crystal, by Carol Scott

I FEEL MORE THAN I SEE

I feel more than I see
Memory takes hold of me

If I touch more than taste
And taste more than see
Will your beauty quell the past
And swell the present for me?

I am here
It is now
You are the divine now
To overcome my then
Grace take hold of me

Time cannot offend
It lacks your love
It has no power to embittered end
You stand above
A ballast of perpetual light
Inconceivable and wise

Aeon cannot compete
You are the inside of dream
The happiest eternity
Every hour redeemed
Spilt time tasted on my lips
Joy of joyful ships arriving at dock
Forever colors that feel more than see
The heart of gold with bright open lock

Tight, tighten
Light, lighten
I can see
Holy Spirit enter me

I feel more than I see
I touch more than I taste
Broken bread into Three

POUND ME INTO YOUR BRONZE

Pound me into your bronze
Whatever shape you crave
A sheet of metal
Thunder when shaken
My invocation to you
In dreamless spire

Frozen in fire

Circe Perdue
Rodin's kiss
Lost wax
My concupiscence
Coiling
Demeriting sound

Triangular arching back
Hero uncontested
Unconfessed
Four thighs
Two backs
Poured into bronze
Intercession tiring

Frozen in fire

Heaven burns the doors of hell
Circe Perdue
Prayer of supplication
Found in you

ACHE

Pray for me and I will pray for you
Longing for justice
Aching for peace
I surrender to you Christ Jesus
That you look with favor on my plea

Trust opposes anxiety
Mercy can be sweet
Acceptance compelling
I kneel before your feet

Always
Sempre
Aeternum
Pray for me and I will pray for you

If I could transfix
Your great aching sorrow
To my body
I would

Again and again
I would

I would twist its resignation against me
And deconsecrate its power over you

I would reconsecrate you in the chaplet
Of our passion

I would be the rosebuds of life itself
Flowing over you

Again and again
I would

I would twist your pain until it is mine
Releasing you from all sorrow
Until the finest drop of your essence
Was freed to roam the earth
And once again you were all lightness

I would take the undiluted you
And place you
In the warmth of my arms

I would hold your life-force
For every second needed
Until your body came back to you
Until your spirit remembered greatest joy

Again and again and again
I would

Don't you know by now
I would do nothing other
Than overcome hell to love you
To love you as perfect as angels

I love you beyond all cause
Only by loving you as you are

Our love could resurrect
Exalted happiness in sunken chairs
Of rolling laughter and red brick home
Covered as lovers do in sacred ecstasy

Again and again and forever again
I would love you
More perfect than angels

Pray for me and I will pray for you
Freed of pain
Released from sorrow
Today and tomorrow

Pray for me and I will pray for you
Trust opposes anxiety
I kneel before your feet
Always
Forever
Tomorrow and the next
Coursing in and out of us
Elation

FIRST SOUL

When I was your little one
Tinier than first soul
The scent of lilac filled every place
And my heart broke with unknowing sadness
Was it for you my Lord?

When all the rays of each color came together to be brightest, beautiful light
Did I see God?

When my voice made sound
Forming words
Singing songs
Would you answer?

When I lifted my hand to caress
Hold and pray
Could it be love?

My soul shivers

THE EIGHTH DECADE: LOVE

"The meaning and worth of love, as a feeling, is that it really forces us, with all our being, to acknowledge for another the same absolute central significance which, because of the power of our egoism, we are conscious of only in our own selves. Love is important not as one of our feelings, but as the transfer of all our interest in life from ourselves to another, as the shifting of the very centre of our personal life. This is characteristic of every kind of love, but predominantly of sexual love; it is distinguished from other kinds of love by greater intensity, by a more engrossing character, and by the possibility of a more complete overall reciprocity. Only this love can lead to the real and indissoluble union of two lives into one; only of it do the words of Holy Writ say: 'They shall be one flesh,' i.e., shall become one real being."

—Vladimir Solovyov, *The Meaning of Love*

Passion, by Carol Scott

I AM THINKING ABOUT THE SMALL OF YOUR BACK

I am thinking about the small of your back
The way the wordless Will
Of your finery
Collects
Exquisite finger bowl

I am thinking about method
And measure and form
Of your downward slope
How it appears to dance
Conform
Bit by bit to a hidden
Intrinsic perfection

I am thinking about your hips
Movement in singular direction
A nascent dip
Puddles I could pop
Your leagues
With my tongue

I am thinking of the angelic order
Of dominions and thrones
How they have no need
For the wrapped sheet
The steamed glass
No backs
No lungs
No sighs in waisted clutch
No golden bones exposed to sun
No streaming condensation
On your panes of glass

Still they exhale throughout eternity
With a reach they have and have not
And we feel them upon us

As I take you on
You take me on

I am thinking of the ways we mourn
The taming animalesque
The naming of unspent years
Shed silk
Fingered tears
The once and final dropped hope
We have bled little
And bled much
These things, such things
Seem to escape my touch

I remember the strings that pulled time apart
I think it was then I felt the you of you
Coming upon me as mastery
All impenetrable velvet

I love that broken open
peach at the sunset of your back
The Creator had too much fun
All too much of the kisses
Made for moving body
When he made you

I can recall being told about dying
Between survival and acceptance
They find a depth of ground

I want to make love
Into our own ground
The thought of your shake with mine
Your pinched lake
Rivulet
Some mischievous angel gave your body
More places to be missed

THE UNCOLLECTED

Long ago
Before the rivers and seas
Formed and dried
Only to fill again
Before the forests were paved in concrete
Before numbers removed and countered
Before stars burnt out
Before you were born

Decades before time
Before cities were made to burn night
Before there were bones and beetles
To ground down in your bowl of tint
Before texture and finger ridges
I promised to shape myself
To the inscape of your body

Before there was the word "surrender"
Before there was language and tongues
I promised to be
The underlying curve of your knee
To my dying day
I would be your feet

Miles before I could crawl
I dragged my half-eaten soul to you

Before elegy and ancestry
Before the first pyre and the first death
I promised
To garland your substance upon me
To be what fits your embrace
To wrap my soul in stars
In winding cloth
My head upon your head

Centuries before one single cell of life
Was given dim sight
I dragged my half-eaten soul to you
Spilt in two but all for you
And you are
Forever you are

I did not know you then
You and I did not exist
Nameless lovers before space and time
I could not breathe
I had no lungs nor beating walls
No altars
No knees
Uncollected dust

My fingers had no hands
There was no fruit pulled apart
No still life on your table
I never dipped my hands in color
No wet hair from rain
Pulled back to gather sight of you

But I made this promise
Before my first thought
Before time knew its cost
Before math unraveled addition
And broke all the clocks

I cannot tell you the promise
You know it
You are
And you are
Forever you are
Within the uncollected dust of me

Before there was earth for dust to settle
Before there was ground to crawl
I dragged my half-eaten soul to you
For you to eat again
And you are

Forever you are
Within the uncollected dust of me

LAGO DI BRACCIANO

If I could assemble myself without defense
Smaller even than innocence
I would be the stem that breaks
The sprig bent underfoot
I would promise you trees and garden paths
If I could make myself last

To be hunted by you
Without the power to resist
To be nothing more than your bee-stung mouth
The fruit still on Autumn vine
I would give you your faith
More than life I would give
I would deliver my soul
Eroded and flowing in your ecstasy
If I could make myself last

I would drain my being into unreflected vessel
Filled and drunk every day that you live
I would promise you hundreds of sailboats
Orange peels, sunsets dipped in tonic
Intoxicants doubled
Smoke perfuming pillows
Bedroom corridors shortened
Your hand on my waist
Tightened into little death
If I could make myself last

You could tow me through water
Undress me in waves
Discard me as olive pit
Forever rolled on your lip

Then I could reconcile your faith
Being nothing other than it
Broken cruelest mystery
Dissolving me into you

Ever without defense

If I could last
Then I would be your faith
If the die were un-cast
I would promise you the exquisite picaresque
The pain that softens sheets
Forever rolled through hips and tide
Drink the wine
Tasting of me
Sleeping on your chest

I would be your awful faith
Your redolence tarries my thigh
Forever lost
A lake undressed into waves
Your tongue to the salt of my cheek
Unpossessed
Given in daylight hue
Emptied vessel poured into you

THE INCARNATE ECSTASY

Edges of evening remake the scene, undress the long sweep of dark
There is but one thing we have, one ruinous beauty that we are. There is but one Word between Us and it has lasted miles and rows of vineyard fields from the beginning of hands in toiled earth Till now

Till this very moment my love the Word between us has lasted

It has lasted plunged with sword into flesh yielding your consummate force of gentleness

Break me down. Break me. Ground me into dust my love

The Word that we are has lasted amid the consumed, hushed, and hollow

Your life has always been on my lips, decades placed upon them. I place my fingers where you Mouthed my name

The Word that lived forever in silence between us is here. Fearful of what it will say or not say, What is said and unsaid. My life has always been on our lips

Break me down. Break me. Ground me into dust my love

Amid the drawn-down lines of night now poured into cups to place upon mantles of memory, and Into our frames . . .

Lay beside us dear Word
Inlay us
Inlaid together within those edges of grace amid the grass

THE COTSWOLDS, MY LOVE

Days long past their due
Renewed in half measure with every passing glance
The Cotswold wedding, only you
Always you

You are the cool autumn rain
The broken stones
The half chill on my cheeks left warmed by your kiss
Far away from the infirmity of age and other
Not yet spent
Unspent
Re-spent on manufactured time

Time to do our bidding once more
One more time
The train's whistle
The church bell
The things that live by setting sun

Time hath snuck its foe inside my throat
It calls your name in my wailing
Every inarticulate happiness finds its way into my face
On my cheeks
Into the softened well below my eyes where tears rest before falling
Unrestored in you
Always you

Concaved chest, the weight of your recollection
You are my dissonance and my innocence
The coursing whispered touch
You have broken my boughs with the folly of your gentleness and grace
Into the shelves and drawers of once was and nevermore

My love you have ruined me in memory
You have taken my sides and lanced them with your affection
Unrepeatable affection

You are parks and city blocks
The small café of life and time
Tea and chatter
Of happy bodies transfixed in pattern

Who shall I be without you?

You who have ruined me with memory
A caramel-colored shell upon the beach
Still as rock
Water approaches and recedes

You are perfumed memory
My intoxicant of sacred things
Cast into the wishing well

OF ANZIO

The sainted immaculate memory of you
Caresses the trees in bloom
It is without trace, it needs no tracing
It is the one single finger ever drawn along my cheek and nape
To take the spun yellow and gold that shrouds my face and lips
Memorizing your face and your lips
Your presence is found in every drawn-up chair

To the table
To the sea
Off we go hand in hand with grit of sand in toe and shoe
This place of breeze and foreign tongue sliding in and out of my mouth
To speak your figures drawn
Your words in shape

I am where those who wait must go
Into the pattern of daily ends
Into the blue more loving than all yielding passion
Into the blues and purples and violet evening light
Into the artist's undisclosed sacrificing sight
The peace forbidden and far beyond the fertile land cleaves to ringing bells

Wake me as you go little spirit of love, mercy, and death
Bound my body and face, make me a substance of grace
Where memory felled the land so long ago
Make a bed of my arm and my legs
Curled in you
In secretive haste, make me a substance of grace

STRAWBERRIES AND CREAM

If tomorrow you were to smile
I would melt in strawberries and cream

I would while hours away
In your pretty feature
Swimming in your sweetness
Floating on happy back
Drinking your smile

Sweet and sly
In the curvature of your eye
One upturned beam
Thoughtless daydream

Tomorrow is still tomorrow
Will there be fountains of you
How I would melt with peaches
And wells of whipping cream
Milk chocolate candied dove
Vanishing into dream

The sky may fall
Heaven on my lap
Crumbles of blueberry pie
Overflowing in cream

Tomorrow is still tomorrow
And today I wait
Fountains of you
Melting my soul in two
Flesh of my honeydew

OF FRIENDSHIP

"I long to see you engulfed and drowned in the sweet blood of God's Son, which is permeated with the fire of his blazing charity."
—St. Catherine of Siena

Oceans meet their end at dried sand
And mountains lose their height
Becoming hills
The rolling hillside caresses itself
Into stretches of farmland
Far beyond eye

Heartbreaking creation
Ready for seed
Eastward morning path among the rows
Of verdant green
Sometimes sun-kissed yellows intervene
Hands at plow young and old
Miles of corn and sunflowers
Brilliant before the altar
Fed on sun and shower

Soon it is fall
The autumnal cower
The lover's call left colder on doorstep
Fireplace and rust
Every year another gain and loss
Sweet suffering loss
The wood crackles into dust
Softening heart
Measured out in hidden time
And quiet tucked away room
Photo and postcard
And quieter roadside memory

The days shorten and fight to regain
The long sunburned step of spring again
The chilled river stirs bones
Blessed are the little ones at play
Blessed are those who see the new day

The Lord and Lamb of land and toil
Know harvest must bring all things to bend
Every movement ceases
And begins another
Every beginning is an end

In all of this
There is nothing simpler, sweeter, and more loving than a friend

YOU SHOULD KNOW BY NOW

You should know by now
That I plan to love you
Better than anyone
Under heaven's own sun

Then as days do come
Know that I know little else
But passion for you made tender
So follow me as I you
I have no joints
I am all things that bend

The tragic netting
Severs forethought
Swoops us up from private depth
Gasping and cinched
Pulling the catch

But better than anyone
I planned to lay my love upon you
As flower blankets field
And snow hushes winter earth

We are two fish
One little and one small
We make our way through
The grated entanglement
Space upon space of hope and love
My beloved who created me

THE LONG NOW

We are permeated and punctured
With caverns and inlets
Of love for the other
I hardly need to find you

I am writing in ways I never knew
Every arena of my being opened
Every ceiling of my soul cracked

I feel the air becoming earth
I feel the earth's plates quake
I feel you breach the center of my earth
All things held in you
My last poem

May I relinquish my word?
My verb has faded
May I fall into deepest sleep?
You've become the word
The tributary of fragrant oil
Rolling smooth upon my back

I sense my own station
Enter the kingdom of your mind
Your sap flows in the roots
That fill my heart
I will burst soon
In love for you

If your fingers could fit into my veins
If you could plunder my heart
It would be all ambrosia
All you
The heart of my last poem

Love: The Shared Poetry of Artist Carol Scott and Caitlin Smith Gilson

Love and Pain, by Carol Scott

HOLY COQUETRY

There will be a holy coquetry
In your canvas of tomorrow
Immune from sorrow
Outlasting fatigue

There will be stairs of paint to your tower
Your lighthouse of shade and shine
Sanctified lineaments laid upon the white
The stuff of dreams
Teeming with bright incarnate waves

There will be a convex of mirrored embrace
Indistinguishable from the artist's face
Unvexed and pure

And in all things you do . . .

There will be your kindly canonized lovers
Cavorting in glass
Long pivots of beveled crystal
Un-shattered till the end of time

Poetry for all seasons
Calling on gods to beguile the muses
Inside dream the vision becomes art

Slake my thirst
Descending god on your knees
Art elevated into poetry
Poetry pressed and shaped as clay
First and final form
Dancing till unworldly and unworn
Shorn and heaved from Olympian cliffs
Holy sanctified coquetry
Entrancing the perfect day
The canvas of tomorrow inside today

TO THOSE WHO DO NOT KNOW

Thank the gods
The incarnate mysteries
The etchings on walls
And all signs, symbols, and contingencies
That she
The one who rivals consummation and ecstasy
Is as river and lake
Smooth and can take
All sky and face lived and denied
Where reflection can be seen

And she gives what she wants to give

She could split rock
Sink ships
Break tide
Command the migration of birds
The wicked beasts at her feet
Her alabaster soles
Smoothing her touch upon the fur

She could unmake charted stars
To shine in daylight streetcar
Twinkling light
Romancing day into night
Evening's transport of serious play
Polyphonic slain heart

She, the necromancer of unearthly delight
The metaxy, the in-between
Baking the clay in her tempestuous ray
Sensuous in silvered slate
Overthrowing every earthly king and queen
Father and Son
Seen and unseen

She caresses the leaves in meadow
Apple blossoms on quieter country lane
Painted portraits and poolside play

And she gives what she wants to give

Ferocious
Wild
Willing the peak and come
Cock and hen
Demanding
Enterprising
Soaked in love
Inebriated in her gentler sex
Records undone

Those who do not know
Fall asleep without dreaming
Those who do not feel
Fall asleep dreamless
Those who do not know
Fall asleep without dreaming

I know and I do not know all the same
What makes her the incarnate courtesy

And she gives what she wants to give

High vaulted ceiling and the violet wall
The climbing window light on easel and canvas
Of morning Mass half nine
Of little things, bleeding, blending
Rubbing the color
Finger and thumb
Rosary bead and hidden need
The blood with the wine, into time
Forever in time

And she gives what she wants to give

Ravenous for living
She writes like breathing air
With perfumed words of wafted wisdom
Graced with ease and beauty clear
No friend could be held so dear
Fathomless soul forever free
Running
Moving in and through Being
Connected to the universe
Standing in charm
More than her legal share
Beloved
And she gives what she wants to give

THE NECTAR OF SWEET DREAMS

You are one compressed breath
Before I lose my life each night
Somewhere among the angels' hum
Rolling bell
Downward spell
You are in me

Upward gaze
Floating in the Milky Way
Star struck in endless moonbeams
Brings the nectar to sweet dreams

The earth has to die each day
For me to catch sight of you
You are my North Star

THE GROUND OF YOU

You are special
Perfect in your imperfections
No other words can take the place of

I love you

Your perfections are many
But I love you because you are you

You have me the unwrapped ribbon

All living and breathing
Every wordless
Missing time
Gravitating

Depth of the ground of you

You have me the uncrated porcelain
Partitioned veil
Lifted kiss
Innocence wept

Into deepening ground of you

You have me the cliff over seas
Shape of you
Fragile congress
Damp clay of your seal
Cooled down upon the body blue

Resting depth of the ground of you
Perfect in your imperfections

IX. THE NINTH DECADE: ROSARY

*"Nothing so beautiful as a child who falls asleep
while saying his prayers, God says.
I have seen the dark, deep sea, and the dark, deep forest,
and the dark, deep heart of man.
I have seen hearts devoured by love
throughout a lifetime.
And I have seen faces of prayer, faces of tenderness
Lost in charity.
Which will shine eternally through endless nights.
Yet, I tell you, God says, I know nothing so beautiful
in all the world
As a little child who falls asleep while saying his prayers
Under the wing of his Guardian Angel
And who laughs to the angels as he goes to sleep.
And who is already confusing everything and
understanding nothing more
And who stuffs the words of the Our Father all awry,
pell-mell into the words of the Hail Mary
while a veil is already dropping on his eyelids
the veil of night on his face and his voice."*

—CHARLES PEGUY, *THE MYSTERY OF THE HOLY INNOCENTS*

Full of Grace, by Carol Scott

I DREAMT OF YOU

I dreamt of you
Until I could not find
The thread back to this life

Running fingers across
Fields of spice and grain
Cut down acres of me

I dreamt of you
Until my soul
Left my bones in bliss
Forever a forgotten thing
A fallen pine comb
A shell of pining love for you

Would you split my dream in two
One half the dying in me
The other half for you
Take the best part of me
Take the half that always calls out
For your midnight hallowed sight
Drenched in your resilient blue

When you split me in half
All of my blood and water flow
Lay down in my dreaming river
Become my place in you
Crack my body open
Take my dreams away
Take what God alone has known
And God had given me
But he has known before time and earth
That I am yours

Your ghost has followed me down the well
And my tongue once split in two
Rejoined in the fire of you

THE SHADOWLESS WOMAN

When did I become pulverized ivory
Soaked up in long Lenten tear

Cascading down

Resting briefly
In the underside of your warmth

Infinite edge
You give and remove me

Why is my skin absorbing the stars
All powerful love
I am stone in sight of you

When did my breathing become coral
Miles below the surface
You give and remove me

You siphon my sex and graft my arteries
God, you make me and make me
Again every morning

I think I am dying because of your love for me
Hurt filled with you
Compressed under your soft embankment
You have weighted me down
Fingered into wooden box
Made of time-flowing confectionery
Sweet
Drapery of you

My heart is impelled inside its soul
It lives beyond its means
Tender infinite edge of pressure and pain
You give and remove me

I am in the shadowless kind of dying
Car after car of passing train
Wailing its steam
I am stone in sight of you

God, you make me and make me
And make me
I cannot bear your force upon me
My head lays against devils crushed underfoot

Between the sheets
Heartbeats
Brain waves
Every record
You give and remove me

VIRGO PERDOLENS

Hushed tenderness nears the end of all good and incomplete ends
Breaks the leaves and twigs underfoot
Rounds the corner of the untroubled riverbend
Seeps as rain into my gloves
To my fingertips
Stokes the memory of old loves
Treads upon fresh snow with a whispered touch
Speaking the name before name
Then stills itself into heartbreak at my front door

Hushed tenderness sits down among my pretty things
Our Lady of Sorrows
Wages her silence into the room
Into the furniture
Into the fire folded into embers
Helpless
One shift and collapse of shape
Is all there Is

Helpless and hushed into tenderness
You, the immortalizing death, knew my time of sorrow had come
You, the wanderlust within innocence and betrayal, cast depth and night as cape upon my face

Hushed tenderness draws the bath and closes windows
A rendered warmth, the dearest of friends
Our Lady of Sorrows, undermine every avenue of my being
Into your sweet resolve, carry me as you break the bondage
Fired and welded into any shape you see fit
I am yours, a child only for you
Forever in you
Forever dying for you

Hush me tenderly within the maudlin blue

ANOTHER FIAT

Tongue-tied wild word
Clarified with wine and falling night
Roll high yet lay low
Rummaging for that last line of my heart
Which can say the many winged things
In one fumbling sheltered word

This flesh of my own soul
Lives pressed against my throat
My wordless self
Tracing the contours of your features for miles
And there is nothing to give you in return
No word or deed
Nor any Will be done

A trodden touch carving its passage into sleep
Into rest darker than night
Obedient to sun and sinless moon, and forever night
My touch lay unrestored
My word never rises to the score
Nothing claims the secret geometry
My uninhabited heart set apart on the shore

We are pieces thrown first as breadcrumbs,
Then as stones
Waves retracting their force from the shoreline
Countless rounded-down pebbles exposed
Dropped into the depth

Long ago before the seas rose
Long ago in days of sun and dappled things
Smoked wafted from balconies
Warmed bread and wine
Today the iron grate lays upon my face
The Madonna of earth and time placed below memory

OUR LADY REMAINS

My body falls apart
Into the ghost of your higher sex
Pristine as veiled blue and cream

A single memory outnumbers me
Finger and thumb
Your Son's body and blood on my tongue
Roses of rosary beads
Lay upon Eden's tree

Repurpose my bones
A heap of wood
Kindling beneath the mantle
How I burn bright
Shot through you
Our Lady of veiled blue

Lay down my body
Lay me down
I am all body and no soul
Ash from coal
Haunted by brooding water

Virgin of virgins
I am all body in need of soul
Nothing heats the coal
Decant my spirit in glass
Ruptured broken host
I cannot breathe
Grabbing mystery as I go

Eternal Mother of the wine and bread
Rearrange the disks of my spine
Reform me into honeycomb
Prisms of dulcet fleshy memory
Impassioned by your Lamb
Both living and dead

Your pierced heart softens rock
Your face presses mine into stained glass
I am not worthy of what your soul can do
Unworthy of your gentler blue

Hold my body
Hold me down
Unmoved in you
All body and soul
Preserved by you
Flexing cache of memory
Font of bliss
Light of veiling blue

CHARA

You are the conception of all ends
The curving heated tenderness that gilded my heart
After the first fear and the first touch
Trembled as leaf in autumn

Little hand on hand of majestic hours and majestic lands
Of secret morning labor poured into being
The gold shines as fire, casts the ring
All things new

You command the virginal aura
The light which plays under and through
Salvaging me with your grace

You pour souls forth into your numinous intensity
Varnished into the crimson shine of blushed roses perfuming the table
Lay me down, my body, into the cruciform three, into you, into ghosts and gods
Forever the convex of tint and wanderlust bliss

Shade my face into the great sleep
Deploy me in your passionate truth
Where beauty remains pure
And ready to break every bough of this tree that grows into my ground
Remain breaking every bone of mine
Snap them as twigs in the morning
When the grass is tall
Break them again
Save me with your beauty

I am not worthy of your incarnate intricacy
Of the shapes you command into life and light
Let there be light
You caress me into the carnality
Of which angels know nothing but longing sighs
Abysmal wells of groaning sighs
You have me in the net of longing

Languishing for the clay and earth
Sweetened with jasmine and warmth plied with shock of spirits

Your beauty must be pushed into my marrow
Split my spine, my femur, every little bone
Find the softened sponged blood of your blood
Hope of your hope
Wreck me with your beauty

Salvage me with your hue as unworldly as steps descending into night
Orion dips with sword thrust
As stars find the moon

You are the confession between beginnings and ends
The laying down of the softest sighs
The aching gentleness of breast and kiss
The wildness of forests forever untouched
A scenery of weeping ecstasy

You are the gift to follow home
The unfolded map in every press of your mouth
You signify the form made flesh
You are the fountainhead of parting breath
At this moment you are the end of time
The moment when knees must drop
For the time being
History and time know nothing but your softest sigh

THE WATERFALL

You have rappelled
Into heaven's low door
As waters rush through
Unafraid reverent passion
Wild calculated action
Un-surrendered to the end

You hold the door frame
Pressing each hand and foot
Toes curled on the lowest angle
The soles of your feet gripped
A mountaineer beyond oxygen
I gasp for you

You have figured a way to take me apart
Piece by piece without causing my death

I gaze far from the low door
Below moon and star
You watch the water that you are

Between purgation and expectation
I cannot reach you
You have split me in two
You are beyond Adam's tree
Which glistens for the few

Your waterfall is loving treachery
Finer than knife cleaving atom
The food of life
The fermented fruit into fragrant wine

The waters of the low door
Move your whole body
Waterfalls surmounting you
But you are the ever-held beauty
The middle ground

Purgatory in wait
Wading ecstasies across your loch
Filling your inside
Water becoming color and tide
Soaking your long dressing gown
Rendering it longer still
Stretching the fabric into cataracts of blue
You are the river around you
Indistinguishable you are from the gown
A trail of Holy colors descending down
Bellowing in the chasm
Of softer unheard word

You have figured a way to severe my throat
I have no speech
My red red roses curling down
But I do not drown

In all your unattested mystery
The water of you
Your gown
Your color
Flowing into soundless earth
Kissing the mortal within me
Of home and hearth
And word made form

You have figured a way to guillotine me
But I still breathe and see
And my heart is now all of me!

Every space I once was
My heart has taken
Flowing out to sea
In your waterfall

My soul remade
With the smallest seed
It grows into jungle

Into forest of fallen rain
Forged in Christ's threefold pain

Impossible you are
In the long dressing gown
Water-coloring the earth
In your image after icon
After image
Flowing out to sea

You have figured a way to bring me to death
Torch me as kindling wood
But my skin is as soft as lamb
And my eyes wet with tear
Flowing out to heavenly sea

MANNA

A fledging blessing in every side-swept glance
It is all can do
To cast my loving affliction over you
Whatever I can do
Will be done
I have cut off my hair
And stripped bare
I am spun cloth and wishing well
Do what you will

I am virgin prayer in downward gaze
In the knowing which does not know
Stir the sugar in the cup
Hold me as worlds come away
As universes tumble in the teacup
Dance me into night
Do what you will

I see the parting of you in squinted eye
But I am left undissolved
My heart once fluttered but it cannot fly
Some unmovable block
Stands in the way
Hold me as worlds come away

Bitter root twists my flesh
The braided regret
Disheveled kisses disturb the ground
My eyes shutter in the psalmist's cry

I lower the veil of my eyes upon your chest
A benediction to your cadence
To the line that separates my breast from you
Seven days
Seven pairs of ribs
On the seventh day let us rest

Let us sleep as worlds burn
I am with the fallen manna among the beads
In rows of sugar cane
High grass covering my sight
Dissolve the drops into my eyes
I have no more tears
But I must weep
And hold you as the world falls away

I will wait in the breadcrumb trail
Meet me in longest day
Never forget
I am stirring the sugar in the cup
As you sleep

Rosary: The Shared Poetry of Artist Carol Scott and Caitlin Smith Gilson

Beautiful, by Carol Scott

THE ROSARY

The Knotted Rope and Chain

The rosary kneads into you
As its pressed into me
Bonding us in a shroud of roses
Estuary of reflected glass

The rosary recites pure love
Pours love into unworthy heart
Pours surrender too
Overflowing even with *Eros*
Filled to the brim
Stretched heel at the altar

How many hands
Have held your knotted rope and chain?
Our Rosary yokes time and agony
Resignation, longing, and pain
Comes upon the soul as waters stilled

How many mortal hearts have passed into you through the needle's eye?

How many dead have you comforted in the grave?

When I rest in pine
Be my light of night
Littlest and surest night light
For children
The eternal light which shines
All the way Home

Flowering Virgin
Bearer of the incarnate Resurrection
Call my name as your daughter
In the darkest day
We hold and pray
As we say

Mary's glow
Scented roses
Ten hails and holy perfect mother
My hand fingering the crystal
One in mystical grace

Glory be
Thanks be to Our Father
I am loved

The Recollection of Angels

Goodnight land of lock and key
Hold my palm in vale of stars
Read my fortune as I dream

I have gone to sleep in the great Love
With arms the length of night
With arms of lamb's wool
Pressed to my dream-lit face

Hugged in deep blue dome
Shooting stars
Comet flaming
Abandoned care
Angel guard standing

I have gone to dream with my great Love
Whose waters flower my forested heart
With arms the length of night
With arms of lamb's wool
Pressed to my dream-lit face

She is honeyed magnolia in repose
Heavy perfumery attracting all the bees

How many hands
Have held your knotted rope and chain?
Slept in your exquisite domain?

I know that I am
Precious
Rarest of all
Fortune's child
Asleep inside your veil of blue

ON CHRISTMAS DAY

On Christmas Day
With angel's song
A Mother was created
Perfected gift to the universe
When Cross was still manger

Virgin veiled
Mary, the flowing sweetness of her breast
All before the earth confessed the dead
Before the cloth is ripped and torn
He, a slumbering life born in hay

The life of the Seven Dolors
Our Lady of Roses
Brought the garden to Bethlehem
First love without thorn

Mother Redemptress
You hold and rock the unborn and born
Cradled child Jesus
Passion's pieta of your embrace

God bringer
Star of the sea
My ship is in roughest water
Rock me in your arms

Cause of our joy
The flowers have gone to sleep
Place your kiss upon me
When time is fatal

Mother of mercy
I am one of your lost sheep
Find me
In the last line
When time is fatal

ROSE OF LOVE

Rose of love
Five-decade garden
Most perfect prayer
Blooms never withering
Bud to full
Wrapped around the world

Chanting Ave Ave Ave

Heaven unclothed its bouquet
Petals drift earthbound
All power and consummation teeming
Dropped into lined beads
Forged glistening tears
As bright as Christening gown

Chanting Ave Ave Ave

Your life of the Lamb
Washed white in veiled weeping
The sawed tree
Cut down
Pressed into coal
Compressed
Into Virgin beads
Decades of love overflowing into me

Mary Mary Mary
Teach me to pray

CRYSTAL FIRE

Our Lady is miraculous innocence
Burning into all things
Embers blown
Shivering into sublime tone
Fugues of atoning violet
Symphony of divinity
Seen and unseen

Our Lady is brighter than freshly dipped cotton
Whiter than blinding shroud
Fallen at the foot of the risen Lord

Our Lady is inviolate innocence
Passion and purpose
Lamb of the broken bread
Contoured to the Cross
Bended head of woven crown

Our Lady is rioting orchids
Under luminescent neon light
Ruby red
Erected prisms
Jackfruit halved
Mandarin flowers flowing precariously
In heated spells of color
At the very brink of steam
Shimmering in beatific color

Our Lady is crystal fire of the immaculate sight
Flame that does not consume
Tongues of light branded on your heart
Holy Spirit domed in color
Swallowing God's Sun

Our Lady is fire, an idea that glows
Blessed, beautiful
Shimmering salvific hues

Miraculous conception
Fused into beams of light
Holy and true

Our Lady is the holiest blue
Who knew color could save
Open the eyes of your soul
Tint of silenced sighs
Lightning strikes
Delighting combustion
I surrender
I am yours
I am light by your fire
Baptized by fire

Our Lady
Make me a saint

X. THE TENTH DECADE: SUFFERING

"The universe screams. The concrete records the violence that's hit it like a wall. The concrete cries. The grass groans under the animal teeth. And Man? What can we say of [M]an? The world is suffering spread out, on display. At its origin, there is a knot of suffering. All existence is an expansion and a crushing. All things suffer until they are. Nothingness vibrates with suffering, until it arrives at being: in an abject paroxysm."

—Michel Houellebecq, "Staying Alive"

Honey Island Swamp, by Carol Scott

ANGUILLARA

Exile me in clean silence
Ransack my heart
Clutch and steal with low-born breeze
All that I am
And will be
Covetous of the sweet insecurity
You rile and remake
Take it all
All that I am
And will be
And never was

Ravage what bones I am
In gaze I cannot see
Roll me against what I will never be
Into morning lighter than air
Claim the nothing that I can give
It is all that I am
Please and pleading
Dear one of all moon and sun
It is all that I am
If only you were a you

I am cleaved in two by gliding spirit
Juniper tree and green spindly leaves
The erotic yew of groaning art
Growling up from winter ground
Infinity of brushed blue
Lay down your heart
If only you were a you

Flowers strewn by you
As offerings of sight
No need to roll the dice
Here lies beauty beyond game
It is all that I am
Forsake its early nothings

Forsake me through you
To what is always old
And forever new
If only you were a you

Happiest I am and yet never will be
To know such pang
At my joy of insignificance and artistry
You have struck my deadened heart
Hidden in caged breast
As clock has hands in time

Confess for me
With me
In me
If only you were a you
And I were sparrow on chimney top
Littler and true
A substance of your grace and gaze
When I was I
And we were we
Faces turned to the Holy Three

The sunrise of face to earth
How could anyone survive this mystical peril
This sack of Rome?
A rape and plunder
Lovelier to willing soul
Stake it all
All that I am
And will be
And never was
If only I was your I
And you were a you and mine

Take off the two pins that pull back my hair
One on each side
Love and loss
Of all that I am
And will be
And never was

Claim my face
Claim the years left
Where my arms can embrace
Take the color of my lips
And the flecks of my iris in brown and green
The flower of my sight
Take it till it is night
I love you as if you were here
If only you were a you

The incommunicable
Opens and closes the garden gate
The breath-take of your undying artistry has
Hurled my heart into lake
I am not I
Give me age and let me die

Come to me passage of haunted time
I am I in the place where I want to die
Living endlessly with you
Days running into paint
Confused and in bloom
Bled through blessings
If only you were a you

DESCEND INTO MEMORY

Burn my heart
With the leaves collected
On the first cold day of fall
Then I'll remember your smell

Cathedral Incense
Earthbound snow
Evaporating
Unnoticed

What can I give you
So that I remember your walk?
Your everyday chatter
Repeated talk
The bend of your hand
When you write

Are you writing me?
Calling me home?
Have you evaporated with the snow?

I cannot recall
The thickness of each leg
The slope of your risen thigh
Your measured stride

I keep forgetting you
The things of you
The places that make you
The give and take of you
The smell of your body as vine
Upon mine

I cannot place your walk
Your talk at the door
Opened to me
Always to me

I keep forgetting
As dew burns up too quickly

The ground is sand
Beneath me
As if life had never begun
Far too warm for the snow
To blanket the ground

I keep forgetting you
The things of you
The places that make you
Broken down caravan of memory
The vines of you chopped down
Burning away

What can I take apart
What price must be paid
To record your face
Turned towards me
A universe within you
Poured into wine
Drunk together
As if life had never begun

What can I devastate
Remake
Interrogate
To recreate the ground
That rocks below your bed

Oh to be a lark!
Singing
As if life was always what you said
Go to bed sleepy head

But the ground is sand
Beneath me
To warm for memory

Why do I keep forgetting you
The smell of you
The color of your worn-down shoes
At the door
Opened to me
Always to me

I am reddened with teardrop
In the jet-black snow
Confused honeysuckle
Growling in my femur
I cannot walk
The bone's cold snap
Everything must go
Burn my heart
Blistered pile of coal

God of Abraham
Descend into memory
Into the time of past forgetting
Be fragrance on folded cloth
Reduce my mind to burning wood
Rising up to you

COURS

There you go hunting the other down
Winding wildness into her
Pulling the tourniquet tighter
Such roughness and heartrending gentleness all the same
Such harrowing love in seas of discontent

My dear sweet friend, every unexpiated tear must fall
Things must fall down
Into depth of unseen ground
Every forsaken thought must take its place in the caverned ecstasy of your heart
Wishing wells of lost time, soaked and broken, long laid out before you
Spreading their limbs as vines

You are
Lonely as cut lilies
You are
Untamed and tender wisdom
Tender and untamed
You are
Ferocity and lightning competing in veiled night sky
Collapsing towers of sand and you

Too much love and so much gentleness
You cannot help but hide

My dear sweet friend, every unexpiated tear must fall
An architecture of ruins is made to be torn and burned, and ground down
The pulp stripped from the cream
Wrap around dream dropped from waist and tide
Ride the dying art of death to its delight
Riots of painted flowers at your gates
Rough volleyed lips in the maze of passion and disaffection

How can one hunt you down, crush you, as hidden as you are?
Sink your teeth one by one, your lover holds on

IN THE WONDERLAND OF LAMENTATION

Body lengths of evening
Lay stretched upon the ground
Swirling in port wine
A phantasm of ruby and smoke
Streets with the skin of snake
Shed into your furious embrace

I sink to the dirt of my lot
Mingling my tears with your dust
Every silent confession caught
Greying the floor
Shed into your furious embrace

The lamb and the lion encircle the other
Fangs bared and ensnared
Long ago Lamentation
Pained maternal faces
Racing agonies thrown to the ground
Here lies the fallen Lord
Dead on the floor
Cover his face
Shed into your furious embrace

Nails cleaved from feet
Insistent raised thigh
Unmade
Un-new
Blood of his feet buckling
Collecting
Bursting cry
Shed into your furious embrace

Heat spills into us
The condensation on glass
Rubbed with finger to your temple
Sweat drops to the floor
Beyond the house of the Lord

Little tomatoes red with heat
Oozed into oil and bread
Crushed and consumed together
Shed into your furious embrace

Sands run through my feet
Banished to the floor
Body and blood of the Lord
The chorus of Mary after Mary
Sunk to the floor
The great loss unrestored
Shed into your furious embrace

You bewitch taste
From the labyrinth of your tongue to mine
All my hopes mollified
My end disarmed and incomplete
Bruised by the floor
Shed into your furious embrace

The God of surrender designed me to bend
He pushed my body to the floor
Pushed my face to the floor
Wrestled me to the ground
Violent in love
Violets and roses at your door
Shed into your furious embrace

LOVE AMONG THE RUINS

This terminal love
Winds its way to cliffside parade
Marched to death by high command
Chalk-written orders on flying sand
Absurd demands in the land of memory

Your embrace fails in its reprieve
Irony rolled up each sleeve
You cannot say the word
There is no word to be said
All is memory
Memorials held down and lower still
My arms cannot hold
My hands too small
This descent is not of the dove

My blood withers the freshly painted wall
Your visitation cleans skull
Carves out my substance and seed
As lantern from gourd
Hollowed love
Decimated love
Fit for worms

My homeless heart
Living but dead on the vine
Pulls itself apart
Plucks its own fruit
Pruned and buckling flesh
Fit for nails
In twilight of harvest moon

Beyond medicine
The weeping lay wounded
Too wound around for succor
Unsweetened by touches
Softer than lamb's wool

Love winds itself down
A toy old and spent
Collecting dust on high shelf

Long leftover love
Plummeting fast as stone
Calcified
Un-clarified
Deadened
Deadening love
My hair goes grey
Eyes pasty, grated yellow
As milk soured at the grave

I have no recourse but to kneel
In desperate knighted shoulder
One sword taps each side
I cannot be at your side in memory
Memory cannot save the day

In the embankment steep in photo
I find myself in the lonelier night's watch
Guarding the gate of my dying heart

In the time of early art
The rhyme scheming mortality
Between you and me
Sends shivers of words in my throat
Dried and parched
The water cannot save
The bread does not break
I am starving from loss of love

Embezzling every scent of your perfume
And breathing nothing
The October air steals
The heated clouds from my mind
Bulbous roots pulled with force
From underfoot

I lay with nothing to give but to be given
Knees aching, aging
Claiming only your loss
Drain the barrel of the last of the wine

There are no knelt gestures
No embodied grace
No Seraphic medicine
Trickling from hidden well
No more little rivers of love and holiness

I am starving from loss of love
Reckless, violent in longing
Where is the balm in every smile of your compassionate face?
Your reserve before Blessing
Take bread on tongue as little bird
Let me take bread on tongue as your little bird

THIRTEEN

This wrathful mercenary
Shakes before the standstill
When the world of stage falls apart
Falling inconceivably apart
Surrendering as surf to gravity

The porcelain has cracked open
A deceiving fruit
Pried into sharpened bones
Rib-caged *memento mori*
Ground under foot

A singular sound howls
A plunging piercing wince
The sole broken open
Your haunting picaresque
One ineluctable wounded sex

A languishing lick of blood
Things stung with past kisses
Kicking the clay into air
And your dowry of habit and time
Blown across my limbs as dust

Stolen tears
None reanimate the years
Draped as demigod before the christening
Poured water upon the head
Undressing you in endlessly remade bed

The earth of my artist's earth
Theorizes that things fallen apart
Only your form and color can abide
Stake in me
Your heart that precedes

There is no relief from your contested essence
No unseen illustration
To hush me in the cradle down
No roads that dip into sun-drenched scene

Tumbling into seas
Needy in crystalline sheen
Redolence sweetened as it meets the blue
Breaks the blue
Things fall apart yet retain your hue

The soles of my feet
Cooled and curled into you
Perfumed with bundles of lavender dried
Limes in ice
Cloudless sapphire skies pouring down

Finger every folly
I am your fool
Calling out from intersecting lines
Washed lighter into blonde
Forever in daylight hue

Un-readied for the season of death
The haunting autumn flaw
The thaw crushed wet underfoot
Things upon things that once fit together
Fall apart

Unsealed and pulled from the seam
I am the fool kissing the cream
Blowing it into air
Imploded ecstasy felling tears
Sold tears

Gall and vinegar on my cheek
Into my mouth burying my lips in my teeth
Forever the fool in the hall of your countenance
Counting on time, on measure, and rule
Nothing more than a wild ravaging fool

ARTIFACT

I wear the gloves
The ones bought
To fit your touch

This afternoon
I will lay them out
Warm on the lawn
Next to me
Flat on my back
Sinking into the grass

What other token can you claim
To govern my affection
Devilish inelegant memory
Purchasing my soul in pieces

I am dying in blades of overgrown grass
Drinking from fingered glove
Vanquished in your subverted blue

Who knew the day would come?
When I would be an artifact
Cuts of grass
Falling into the vale
You knew it could not last

ALGORITHMS OF IMITATION

Algorithms of imitation
Close but it will never get there
Never will it smoke another's cigarette in bed
Nor take the hand happily led

It is a double
An imposter
A drizzling delighting fantasy
A lie sliding down
Both sides of the sheets
Cooled in calculation
Lost in translation
Simpering sign of life

Uncreating imitation
No vitality or passion
Nor consecration
The expectation paled
Face as white as bone
Failed to stand
Legless ghostly lust
Dead at the door

MY NEEDY HEART I WEEP

My needy heart
Partially formed

Too small for its own good
Is drenched in sorrow

It feels cold

As heavy gown
Caught in storm

I WILL NEVER LOVE LIKE THIS AGAIN

When the earth fell from the sky
And all the ground was bruised with stone
I was in your arms
Fastened into perfect sleep

You were gravity
You pulled me into you and held on
As I slept
And dreamt of the nothing
Sweeter than all dream

I never heard the earth break apart
I never felt the upturned soil
Give its bodies back to fire and ash
It was you through me
The sadness in my sleep
The wisdom
The ruins
The peace
The pure elixir
It was you through me

I will never love like this again
The earth will not fall from the sky
Water is not wine
Time cannot cancel time

I will know life stretched terminally apart
Every bruise will ache
I will feel the stoning, the icy reach
And I will dream and dream
Violent burning liquor of my dying heart
It was always you shot through me

GOD I MISS YOU

God I miss you
The smell of the rainstorm anchors me to you
And I cry for you
I cry out for you more than I did yesterday

I miss you terribly when the rain comes
When it is about to fall

Today, will it shake the house?

God I miss you
Haunted with awful knowledge
I miss the side of your face
I miss the place where your chin
Curved into your lower lip

I wish my heart would break
Would shatter into finer shards of glass
Becoming embedded at my quick
Pain under fingertip
Unable to be removed
Soaked in rain

Did I tell you how much I miss you when the rain begins to fall?

But my heart keeps itself together
Moving in hidden concert
Stubborn callous survival
My heart keeps moving on
Hateful little thing keeping me alive
Loving thing that it is
Keeping me

I wish the rain would come again
I want you to kiss me and kiss me
Patternless embraces
Except that you would be my constant

Soft and wild

My shoulders and body ache
Everything aches
I wish the rain would hit the windows
Till they break
But my heart keeps moving on

God I miss you
If only the rain would make its way
Into my home
If only my roof were made of metal
And everywhere the echo of you
In the teardrop falling now

Suffering: The Shared Poetry of Artist Carol Scott and Caitlin Smith Gilson

Pushed and Pinned, by Carol Scott

THE RAMPARTS

You feed my ego
Unleashed and ravenous
A Colossus bestride the harbor
Standing over the moon
Monstrous in play
Towering in consequence

Between your legs
The city of divinity falling into flesh
Angels stripped of wing and crown
The Cross nowhere to be found
Unpolished rough wood
Rotting under the waterline

Guard the city gate
Breach the ramparts
All the Greek gods dying in your arms
Paying the price of admission
The heaviest of fines
Hades fleeing his commission

Eternal life demands your mind
Your art of reverie
The silent world of inner spaces
And I, the godless, will forsake you
Swimming between stone legs and untruth
Into storm after soul after storm after you

Little one of sums undone
Forsake your netting
Dropped to ankle's depth
There is no snare or trap
Neither deep nor wide as it seems
The salt has not lost its savor
In the water's edge lashing the middle tree
The lamb undivided in three
Calms the Sea of Galilee

SEVENTY SEVEN

I want a body that can run
I want a body that can swim
I want a body that can crash into the other
Bang and lay and prostrate in savaged seduction

But my mind is better
Better than it has ever been
I know what love is
Dear God of gods
I have known what love is

You can douse my body in spirits
In liquor dripping down the glass
It is all about sight
Not about dream

I miss my body being so carefree
Now I have the weight of the world
Shoulders older
It only gets heavier
That's Reality tweaking time
Let me speak in rhetoric
Ageing crime
Creeping upon the mind

I want a body that does not revolt
I want a body that cannot tell time
I want a body that can dive into lake
Split the water in two
Fresh and new

WAR ON ME

The slings and arrows of a tortured soul
Cruelest suffering
Suffering without reason

How could you want war?
How could you ask for the razor
Sharpened at your sides?
Why me?

You think you can love as Christ loves
Foolish love that you are?

No one wins in war
But who said life is peace?
Meaningless
Demeaning stupidity
Enemies at every gate
Stabbing the soul
Curdling the body
Every expectation too late

I am in the fire that cannot consume
And the greatest sadness of them all
Is not knowing the All

Your love is fool's gold
Promising happiness
Torrents of anguish
When did you nail me down
Where is the bed of my youth?
Why me?

How could I think that I can love as Christ loves
Foolish love that I am?

You promised the Good
But never told me

That it walks with a limp
Dragging its hind quarters
Emaciated hungering pain
Too weak to defend itself
Torn apart by wolves
Thieves and imposters

I am in the fire that cannot consume
And the greatest sadness of them all
Is not knowing the All

You promised the True
But your love fills my heart with cordoned sighs
I cannot perfuse my heart
No winding tourniquet
To stop it from bleeding out

How could you think that we can love as Christ loves
Foolish love that we are?

DESPAIR

The pithy power of ignorance
Madness in stupidity
Sinful arrogance
Egomania
No brainier
Self-indulged
Self-proclaimed

How can one despair
When held in glorious body
The body of life?

Human nature without God
Man needs grace
Man needs God

Do tell
Drunk
Drugged out
Burst soul
Lost

Absolution . . .

Come out of your pity party
Get off of your wheel

Are you made in the image of God?

How can one despair
At the window of intelligence
At the fruit of Being
At the innocence of the child?

Too much poisoned chatter in the breeze
Jointless knees
Catatonic willful pleas

A litany of lies which breed and breed
Heavy dull-witted cruelties

False friends
False loves
Falsities and ill at ease
Idols and idiots

Blown seeds
Scattered on concrete
Reeds and reeds of God's tonic
Confused as weeds

We bury God
Through every century
Under God's own Son
But he keeps rising
Comprising sanctuary
Eat this bread and drink this wine

Made in love
Love remaking love
Making life again
Body and blood

Do not despair
Suffering is grace
If strips us to nothing
But gives us our face

Until we have faces
We cannot see God

Until we have faces
We cannot love another

Until we have faces . . .

We are leaky vessels
In knee depth drowning
Put one knee on the ground

And then the other
Pray to the great lover
Do not despair

You are made in the image of God

Lagniappe

"A gift of any kind is a considerable responsibility. It is a mystery in itself, something gratuitous and wholly undeserved, something whose real uses will probably always be hidden from us. Usually the artist has to suffer certain deprivations in order to use his gift with integrity."

—Flannery O'Connor, *Mystery and Manners: Occasional Prose*

The Big Catch, by Carol Scott

INNAMORATI

by Carol Scott

Beauty
Grace
The lovers embrace
Flesh to flesh
Locked
Licked
Abiding faith
Consubstantial with the other
I am around you
You are in me
Perfected hug
Ultimate kiss
Touched
Touching
Bliss

SLEEP IN HIDING

by Carol Scott and Caitlin Smith Gilson

I would take every last strand of me
Make myself separated, individuated
Countless plucked golden strings
Off-white winter coat
In blinding bright snow
If that is grace you need
If that is what it took

I would make mission of my body and soul
I would watch the blessings depart
Without resistance
Without knowing
The golden sunshined locks of me
Flying and descending

I would take every last strand
Converted mind and body
To wind-blown string
Unable to resist one gust
One half ounce of pressure

If that could be the final act
The consummate bargain
The hand given over
That brings you to life
I would
A thousand times I would

Then where would I be?

I would weave the strands of you
into the strands of me
To cover us in our love

Knot our bodies
Connect our veins
Blood pumping in rhythmic passion
In the flow
We would know
Two into one

We would become cathedral
Candled wax
Stained stones
Jasmine-plied lavender
Pulsed incense
Threaded reams

Peering into you
I'd know nothing of myself
Your eyes
Lashed shined sable
Ascending
Pyrotechnics illuminating
The night sky
The starry night is over all

SEMPRE

by Carol Scott and Caitlin Smith Gilson

The forever one
Peels the skin from the sun
Yet her fingers do not burn
It is Eden again

We are our bodies
The receivers of pleasure and pain
Constant
Insistent
Resistant flesh

The carrier of memories
Genetic code of ancestors
Made better
Worn worse by choices made
Judged by the world

Laughter
Stripped down sorrow
Nothing clear-cut but bodies in motion
A line of dwindling reanimating luck

Divine love squeezes the pulp out of glass
Makes the first things last
Forever
Living on sun-kissed lips
Lifted
Enticed by you
It is Eden again

A living thing
Running in circles
Or stranger straightened lines
Making progress or marking time

The forever one squeezes the pulp out of glass
Makes the last things first
But her hands are spotless
She need not bleed

Transport your heart
Into my body
Into my newest chest
Precious silver and gold
It is Eden again

ADVICE FOR THE BROKEN HEARTED

by Carol Scott and Caitlin Smith Gilson

It may be a wasted sin
I did not come
The door was only slightly parted

Unhappily told
Your prince is a toad

It is not a sin to dream
How perfect you would be
If you were different
If your frame fit mine

But there is no sin in dreaming
Transpierced by Cupid's bow
Pricked by his arrow
Moonlit cadence
Bedding joy

Tonight I thought of you
In my happily ever after

Your actions are the bizarre
A paper tiger growling in chains
Put a bag over your brain
Enjoy your body all the same

It is not a sin to dream
How perfect you would be
If you were different
If the game were not in play

BANANA MOON

by Carol Scott and Caitlin Smith Gilson

Life is not a bargain
Life is not a trade
But you volley it back to me
Expecting a raid upon the heel
When I am getting it anyway
Getting it for a steal

Ice melting in tumblers
Tumbling down
Toss of lemon-colored bribes
And I am getting it any day anyway

Side deals can't be made on loving ground
When her ceilings are heaven's lounge

It is just for us
Two friends sharing your pitch
I catch
The adventure continues
The rabbit did not go down the hole
The hare is in the magician's hat

In Carol's Metairie
Nudes circle the block
A hundred meters back
For a spot on her painted cot
Not a blue moon
Or full moon
Just laughter from dusk till noon
Even in monsoon....
There shall be stripped ditties and poetries

We are the bee's knees
Better than blue suede shoes

Magical pairing
Under the banana moon

Hope we made you laugh
I know we made you blink
Even if it's not a cause to think
But thinking was never the missing link

Friendship and love together
Claim the hidden knot
The tie that binds
Your laughter and kindness
Lifting the canopy of trees
So that I can see the blooms
Lit by our banana moon

THE WHITENED TEAR

By Carol Scott and Caitlin Smith Gilson

At some point in life
The earth reminds you of its power
It exists beyond reason

Terrible power
Centuries of terrible commands
Terrible deeds
Terrifying evils
Banalities and cowardice
Wormed up spirits inside slips
Where is the warrior?

We would lose our consciousness
If we could understand evil
We would lose memory

Torn up folded up vagabond
Of shelled out loaned out lies
Garbage minds eating minds
The world has clogged my ears
The noise of it

We walk upon the ground of bodies
Bodies
Bodies turned to ground
Rot of the wood
Not ash
Utterly forgotten
Where are their souls?

Don't tell me of heaven
I cannot understand
Who can claim to understand
And be honest

Who can claim to understand?

Running
Stumbling
The devil of shade is at our heel
All soul convulsing
Chasing tomorrow

But then God help us
God too cruel too gentle
You come upon us quiet and unexpected
You give us untranslated love
Insignificant to any other
Outside that chain
Outside the embrace

The body was made to be nourished
The body was made for rest

And it is all good
All significance
The whitened tear
Too good
And it conquers
As it soothes

That love could shudder all loss
That love is warmest grace
Too beautiful
The whitened tear
Of your perfections
All seasons held in one

Still, love is left outside reason
How can we survive
Love is not magic
Who can endure
The broken-down
Dying engines of every dream
Dreamt for all time?

It would take some great God
Some terrible dying
No place to go
Finding God
Into the soul
To survive

The body was made to be nourished
The body was made for rest

I love your love
I die a little each day
I will die each day that I love you
And yet live so much more
You take the Cross
And make it Sprig
When we love

Whitened tear of my walled up tear
Your love could remake all design
And so we hold on

Chasing today

UNMAPPED

By Carol Scott and Caitlin Smith Gilson

You have drawn my tongue
Into yours as rolled map
I would collapse if you let me

Your embrace is collision

Your body is piping unsliced pie
Puckered sucked sugar cube

I hope you feel yourself tremble
My fingers read the braille of your body

Whatever you want
I want

I think of your body as your soul
I think of you
Unrolling the map
Your skin
It has no dress rehearsal

The adventure travels on
Both fast and slow
Inner thigh
The story is told
With kisses all over and over and over
Your body my soul
Your soul my body

PURGATORY

By Carol Scott and Caitlin Smith Gilson

Puzzling as a Rubiks cube
Sounds like an organ fugue
Of anxious thoughts and frustrating doubts
Hope is corroding like rusty nail
Pale emptying

I feel bad

SOS

Am I the guiltless or the guilty?
Or do we all reside somewhere in the middle?
Purgatory
Neither sinking nor swimming
In need of the life jacket of the other
The good of the other

All the mixed up shadows of the soul
All the colors combine
Expectation broken, remade, broken again
All the fleeting time flowing below the doorway
We leave our recollections at the great collection

Many temptations
I have succumb
Piper paying time
Of consequence and owing
The feather will balance the scale

Lessons learned . . .

Of gates to heaven opening and endless bliss

THE LIGHT IS TOO BRIGHT

By Carol Scott

Cannot see
the light is too bright
Sun-lit glare
the wisdom of being
You will be seen
Time will show
All the way to be yourself
Enduring and knowing

I love to see a fire fly
You are the light well carried
Seeking seeing
Others see
Creation of magic
Nature fire burning without consuming
And just like this
Destiny comes
Sunglasses required

Air sweet
I breath the scent of roses
You are the air perfumed
My senses are on high alert
And when the surprise awakens
Parachutes open
Grounding gently in reality

ANOTHER THEBAN CYCLE

By Caitlin Smith Gilson

I: The Now

"To love" is another verb for pain
You've known and you have lived it
What can I say but I love you
And your sorrow is mine
Affection so sweet
It could make me cry
Should I let it

But tonight I think
Of all the roads we must travel
And all happiness coming to us
Bigger than winter
More lasting than sound
Recorded and played
Again and again yet unworn

Your heart is that recording
I will play it over and over
Loving you and our precious time
And your joy is mine

II: The Presence

How your wrists are small
As small if not smaller than mine
How can we not glance time?
How can we not be wounded
By the way age
Rummages through us
Lost and found

Every motion in life combines the opposite
The perfect contraries pulled together
These poles sweep the ground
Clear the fields of the little flowers
Leave glasses in the sink for another day
Another way
But there is only one way home

Minds, wildernesses of thought
Bodies tiring, gaping soreness
Suffering as the great lover
Suffering as the kiss that lasts
Death in every life
Found in every gift
Every surprise under the tree
Utterly free and entirely fated

Your wrists remind me of these things
Your hand becoming your arm
Your arm to your chest
There is only one way home
Into the heart of you
Recorded and played
Unworn

III. The Missing

What lies below surfaces
Memories
Enchantments
Entanglements
Keeping us enchained

The torn ticket
The day that never was
The sun fallen down
The groundskeeper of secret
Raking the leaves over the grave

The harbor town
The winding lanes
The night of perfect rain
Ethereal majestic birds
Angels drinking rain

Somewhere time stands instead of you
It stands in your place
It stands in place of you
The eternal bridegroom
Watching my life blown through
The lowest door

The blessing of the dead
The last breath
The easy chair
The sun rising somehow west of you

What can I do
What word is there to resurrect
The simple day
The forgotten happy glorious day
Where nothing happened but you
You happened that day
The sun keeps setting East of you

I lost my compass in the fall
I kept it too close as I passed through fire
I forgot how to learn
I forgot word
I keep receiving pieces of you
I am living on the crust of bread
And the moon never sets

The table is as it was
The chairs still pulled aside
All of your weight weighted down
All of you on my chest but your body
All of you but my soul
I keep re-conceiving these pieces
Setting them on the table

Placing them at angles
Trying to make them fit
Pieces of an unfit puzzle
All of you everywhere but here

IV: The Fool

What if I did not want a heaven
Purged of heartache
What if I desire my tears to bake
To take on the scent of you forever
The heat pressing memory into matter
A stamp upon the mind

What if I cannot take a life of the spirit
I am all surrendered knowledge
A fruit on a vine
All feeling caressing feeling
A willful muscled deathless howl
Over centuries stretched across my touch

I don't understand your heaven
Your peace, your rest
I am wilder with grief and life
Your blood and water torment
They do not teach
How can I long for what I do not understand?
Why are you aging me, killing my flesh
And I cannot know
I will never know what makes you
How can I desire you without my touch?

Merciful God
I do not understand you
I cannot know you
If I am to live I need your pressed lip
I need touch and hold and clasp
I do not want rest unless I am held
I don't want thought without affection
I want the nursery of things

The nestle
I want you as child
All soft cheek upon me
How can I desire you without your touch?

V. The Paradise

Little one
You have no idea of your words
You have no idea what touch is
What touch was before it lost itself in lie
And almost everything is lie
Half upon halved truths
Never enough selfless love
To love truly in return

All the swords of my heart
Pushed through the universe of each and every one of you

Nothing in life ever shakes the dust
One's heart rarely lays bare
Everything is curled in snakeskin
Rusted partial dried up loves

Truth is the first virgin and the last
The last light in your dying
One must know the other
Inhabit the very essence of the lover
Don't you know that you
Must be good enough to be known
To be inhabited completely
To be the grace for another
Filled with the very tears of you
And you filled with their weeping
Each an estuary of the other

All the swords of my heart
Pushed through the universe of each and every one of you

If you knew what touch is
If you knew what truthful love is
You would want paradise
And rest
And sleep
And peace
If you only knew my little one, my love
You would run to me
Every leg would break
But you would run to me all the same

If you find rest on earth
You have stumbled into a little heaven

If you find peace on earth
You have discovered a corner of heaven

If you find love on earth
You have found your heaven

All the swords of my heart
Pushed through the universe of each and every one of you

Night Heron, by Carol Scott

POSTSCRIPT

"*It is also good to love because love is difficult. For one human being to love another human being: that is perhaps the most difficult task that has been entrusted to us, the ultimate task, the final test and proof, the work for which all other work is merely preparation. . . . Loving does not at first mean merging, surrendering, and uniting with another person (for what would a union be of two people who are unclarified, unfinished, and still incoherent?), it is a high inducement for the individual to ripen, to become something in himself, to become world, to become world in himself for the sake of another person; it is a great, demanding claim on him, something that chooses him and calls him to vast distances. . . . Merging and surrendering and every kind of communion is not for them (who must still, for a long, long time, save and gather themselves); it is the ultimate, is perhaps that for which human lives are as yet barely large enough.*"

—Rainier Maria Rilke, *Letters to a Young Poet*

PIETA

By Carol Scott

My son's name was Jesus
He saved the world
A man that was God
God that was man

Honeysuckle memories baby mine
Cuddles and coos all loving you
Then it was time . . .

I was screaming thunderous cries
Don't hurt my son
I am on the Cross with you
Mother and child
Have mercy
Savior save me

Pity on my broken heart
Scared Heart stop the bleeding
Let me rise with you
I don't care if it takes four days or five
Let me rise

Our Lady of Souls, by Carol Scott

The Authors

www.ingramcontent.com/pod-product-compliance
Lightning Source LLC
Chambersburg PA
CBHW031900220426
43663CB00006B/699